A Devotional Guide to

JOHN

The Gospel of Eternal Life

Other Books by John Killinger

A Devotional Guide to Luke: The Gospel of Contagious Joy
A Sense of His Presence. The Devotional Commentary: Matthew
His Power in You. The Devotional Commentary: Mark
Bread for the Wilderness, Wine for the Journey: The Miracle of Prayer
  and Meditation
All You Lonely People, All You Lovely People
For God's Sake, Be Human
The Centrality of Preaching in the Total Task of the Ministry
Hemingway and the Dead Gods
The Failure of Theology in Modern Literature
World in Collapse: The Vision of Absurd Drama
Leave It to the Spirit: Freedom and Commitment in the New Liturgy
The Salvation Tree
The Fragile Presence: Transcendence in Modern Literature
Experimental Preaching
The Second Coming of the Church
The 11:00 O'Clock News and Other Experimental Sermons

The Word Not Bound: A One-Act Play

A Devotional
Guide to
JOHN
The Gospel of Eternal Life

John Killinger

WORD BOOKS
PUBLISHER
WACO, TEXAS

Contents

Introduction

The Gospel of John, almost every one agrees, is special. It is different from the other Gospels. Even the most casual reader senses its uniqueness.

Its picture of Jesus is more exalted than that in other Gospels. There is no narrative of a humble birth, as there is in Matthew and Luke—instead, the prologue speaks of the pre-existence of Christ. There is no "Messianic secret" as in Mark—Jesus is openly and uncontestably the Son of God. There is no prayer of submission in the garden—Jesus goes to the cross triumphantly, calling it the hour of his glorification.

There are no parables in John. Instead, there are numerous "signs" and wonders, often followed by long discourses in which Jesus reveals great eternal truths. In some of these discourses are the famous "I am" statements of John—"I am the bread of life," "I am the light of the world," "I am the resurrection and the life," etc.— that help to characterize Jesus as superior to Judaism and all other religions.

There is much more material in John about the Last Supper— especially about what Jesus said to his disciples at the Supper. The comforting words about life after death, often read at Christian funerals, are part of this material not found in any other Gospel.

The Gospel of John is more sacramental than Matthew, Mark, or Luke. It does not speak directly of the church or allude in specific terms to the sacraments, but its entire background is the

Beloved Community, and it refers repeatedly to water, bread, and wine. It is the only Gospel in whose passion account Jesus' side is wounded, producing water as well as blood, thus suggesting the interrelationship of baptism and communion.

In John, there are allusions to the Holy Spirit not found in the other Gospels. The Spirit will lead disciples into truth, says Jesus (16:13). The Spirit will also be present to comfort and guide disciples when Jesus is no longer present with them in the flesh (14:26).

And, last but certainly not least, John is characterized, far more than the other Gospels, by an emphasis on eternal life. At times, in the Gospel, the phrase seems to refer to life after death. At other times it clearly pertains to life in this world. Taking all the passages together, they speak of a kind of life, known to the disciples of Jesus but not known generally in the world, in which believers are transcendent over all powers that afflict them in this life, up to and including death itself.

The internal evidence of the Gospel suggests that John was not written to convert outsiders but to support the faith of those who already believed. Just as Jesus sent the disciples of John the Baptist back to him in prison to say, "Look around you at all the evidence of my being the Christ," so the entire Gospel of John is composed to remind believers, some of whom may have been in prison as the Baptist was, that their faith was not misplaced.

What an important Gospel it is for our own day!

We too, like the early Christians, live in a world of conflicting loyalties and petty deities where the figure of Jesus should be more exalted. It is necessary to remember his humanity—he was one of us in every way—but it is also important to remember his glorification. This is the only way we can keep the great unrest of our time in proper perspective and not be overwhelmed by it.

We too need to be more aware of signs and wonders—to see what God is achieving in the world around us. Even in the churches there is often a reticence about miraculous events, visions, and healings. God's people languish in their faith because it receives too little mutual confirmation.

We too are hungry for comfort about death and the afterlife. We have allowed scientists and skeptics to erode our belief in the soul's survival, and consequently fear death as much as pagans do.

There is a connection, as the Gospel suggests, between this erosion and our low view of the church and its sacraments today. If we had a stronger sense of community with other believers, and a greater reverence for the sacramental aspects of the community's life, we would not have lost our confidence in Christ and the life beyond death.

By the same token, we need reminding of the Spirit's presence to lead us into truth. We are constantly bombarded by the media. There is more information and less truth around today than at any other time in the history of the world. Most of us don't know what we really believe. If we could only lay hold on the Spirit—or be laid hold of!—it would give us meaning and direction in a confusing world.

Finally, we desperately need, as the early Christians did, a sense of eternal life. Not only for assurance of the future, but for living today. Christians have lost the sense of triumph that is able to turn darkness into victory. We have forgotten how to live joyfully. But here is a Gospel that says to us, as Jesus said to Mary at the tomb of her brother, "Stop your weeping!" For it exalts One who is the Resurrection and the Life, the Living Water, the Bread of Life, the Beautiful Shepherd, the Door of the Sheep, the True Vine.

These things are written, says the author, "that you may believe that Jesus is the Christ, the Son of God, and that believing you may have life in his name" (20:31).

The Gospel does not identify its author by name. Tradition says he was John, the son of Zebedee, and probably also the "beloved disciple" mentioned in 13:23, 19:26, and 21:20.

For many years, this tradition was questioned. Scholars doubted the historicity of the Gospel because it differed so much from the other Gospels. They claimed to see Hellenistic ideas in it, and believed the prologue (1:1–18) was derived from Platonic philosophy. Many thought, because of references to Jesus' flesh and incarnation, that it was written to combat a form of heresy known as docetism, which taught that Jesus only *appeared* to become flesh.

Since the discovery of the Qumran scrolls in 1947, however, all these speculations have had to be revised. Comparable materials from a Jewish community in the second century A.D. indicate that John was indeed a Jewish Gospel, not a Greek Gospel. It is, in fact, probably more intensely Jewish than the other Gospels. And, while the author may have taken some swipes at docetism, the real intent of the Gospel was to encourage Christians who were under pressure from non-Christian Jews to convert to Judaism. This is why the

Gospel frequently refers to "the Jews" and not to "scribes and Pharisees" as the other Gospels do. The author was not refighting Jesus' battle with the self-righteous Pharisees; he was fighting the present battle against Judaizers who sought to destroy the faith of Christ's "little ones," including many Jews who had been converted.

There are some evidences that the Gospel had more than one author. The prologue is written in poetic form and uses theological terms such as Word (*Logos*), grace (*charis*), and fullness (*pleroma*), not found again in the Gospel. There are apparent inconsistencies in the order of material in the Gospel. In 14:31, for example, Jesus concludes his remarks to the disciples at the Last Supper and gives the order to depart; yet these words are followed by three more chapters of discourse, and he and the disciples do not go out until 18:1. In 20:30–31, the author clearly draws the Gospel to a close; but this is followed by another chapter with yet another conclusion. This chapter (21) is different in stylistic details from previous chapters. And, in addition to all of this, there are certain repetitions of sayings in the discourses which seem to indicate the inclusion in the Gospel of two different traditions of the same sayings.

Although this may sound puzzling, it is all very easily explained. John the Apostle, the son of Zebedee, the beloved disciple, doubtless became the leader of a band of Christians, as did most of the Apostles. He delivered his image of Christ and Christ's teaching to his own disciples, probably over a period of several decades. Eventually either he or one of his disciples wrote down an account of the ministry and teachings of Jesus. The author may have known early versions of the other Gospels, and so may have chosen to stress materials different from the ones they emphasized. Then, at some later date, another disciple undertook to edit the original Gospel of John, adding to it other materials he had received from the tradition as John delivered it.

So John, whether or not he actually wrote every word of the Gospel himself, is in reality the author of the book attributed to him. It was his vision of Jesus, his knowledge of actual details, that made this remarkable Gospel possible. The Gospel was as fully his as any book is its author's today when editors, typesetters, and proofreaders have finished with it.

As the scholars for a period took John away from us—or at least cast doubts on the value of his reports—now they have given him back to us. It is a wonderful and timely gift. We have never stood more in need of what this Gospel has to teach!

You are in for a special treat if you read the Gospel faithfully each day, studying and meditating on the passages as indicated in this guide, and then waiting quietly in prayer for the meanings brought to you by the Spirit. You will find, as others have already discovered through the centuries, that it is in some ways the most spiritual of all the Gospels, and that the risen Christ who comes to his disciples in the upper room (20:19–29) will come to you as well. I know. It happened to me as I worked on these pages.

JOHN KILLINGER

WEEK 1

Week 1: Sunday

John 1:1–18   Jesus Is the Light

Word, light, power, grace, truth, glory, fullness. Like the overture to a musical play, the prologue of John's Gospel gives hints of all the themes to be developed later. It is a tremendous introduction—one of the greatest poems ever written. Frederick Buechner once called it "a hymn to perform surgery with, a heart-transplanting voice."

John knew he was writing nothing less than the story of a new creation. His words "In the beginning" instantly recall the opening of the Book of Genesis. The other Gospels—the Synoptics—emphasized the continuity between the ancient prophets and Jesus. John went further; for him, Jesus was the Word that existed before the creation of the world itself!

The good news in John is that this exalted, pre-existent Word became a human being. Let those who believed the flesh is evil think again—the Word was not ashamed to enter it. The redemption of the world would not be accomplished by divine fiat, but would come from within creation itself. Again and again, John underscores the humanity of Jesus. Even though Jesus is the eternal Word, the creative spirit of all life, he grows tired, shows anger, weeps, loves, becomes hungry and thirsty, and suffers on the cross.

Ancient Jewish writings—notably Job, Proverbs, the Wisdom of Solomon, Baruch, and Sirach or Ecclesiasticus—portrayed a spirit called Wisdom that comes from God, dwells among human beings to bring them to the light, then returns to God after being rejected in the world. John sees this spirit of wisdom in Jesus, who is the "true light," yet is rejected even by his own people, "the Jews."

The brightest note in the prologue, after the coming of the eternal Word, is that some have accepted the light and become children of God. These are born, as John says, "not of blood nor of the will of the flesh nor of the will of man, but of God" (v. 13).

These words are a key to the purpose of the entire Gospel. After A.D. 70, when the temple was destroyed, Judaism became stricter in the synagogues. A reformulation of the so-called Eighteen Benedictions resulted in the last benediction's becoming a curse on all heretics, aimed especially at Jewish Christians. Christians who attended the synagogue had either to leave or curse themselves publicly. We can imagine the dilemma this posed. Jewish Christians had grown up worshiping in the synagogues. Now they must choose between Christ and their familiar places of worship.

The Gospel of John was written primarily to encourage Christians—particularly these Jewish Christians—not to renounce their faith in order to be accepted in the synagogues. The Jewish people were born of flesh and blood—"of the will of man." But the children of the light are born of God. Moses, who never saw God, conveyed the Law. But Jesus, who not only saw God but came from the very bosom of God, brought grace and truth.

What more ultimate word could be spoken? Jesus was the very essence of the covenant God had made with his people in the beginning of their relationship. He was *word, light, power, grace, truth, glory,* and *fullness.* He fulfilled every promise God had ever made to the children of Israel.

O God, this is indeed a hymn for performing brain surgery! I feel that my mind is being carried beyond its limits, and I am shown mysteries too great for me to comprehend. I can only bow my head and worship you, content in the knowledge that your light will lead me to salvation, through Jesus Christ, the same yesterday, today, and forever. Amen.

Week 1: Monday

John 1:19–28   The Testimony of John

It is apparent from various evidences in the Gospels that there was rivalry between the disciples of John the Baptist and the disciples of Jesus. This may seem ridiculous to us, but imagine their situation. In an ancient country where communication was poor, they followed itinerant rabbis whose paths seldom crossed. Isolated and limited in perspective, each group of followers respected its own leader as the most important figure in the world. Even after the deaths of John and Jesus, a spirit of competitiveness continued to exist among their disciples.

The author of the Gospel wished to clarify the matter at once. The Jews sent a delegation from Jerusalem, he said, to ask John the meaning of what he was doing. The delegates were priests and Levites, persons intimately acquainted with ceremonial law, including the ritual of baptism. "Who are you?" they asked. John said, "I am not the Christ." The language here is significant. Literally, the Gospel says that John "confessed, he did not deny, but confessed" that he was not the messiah. In other words, John vehemently denied that he was the messiah.

The words John used, "I am not the Christ" (*egō ouk eimi ho christos*), besides being emphatic, foreshadow a series of "I am" (*egō eimi*) phrases used by Jesus later in the Gospel—"I am the bread of life," "I am the light of the world," "I am the door of the sheep," etc. Surely no disciples of John the Baptist could miss the point—their master strongly denied that he was the Savior of Israel.

"If you are not the messiah," the delegation wished to know, "who are you? Are you Elijah or the prophet?" Baptism was an eschatological symbol—a sign of the end of all things. Popular belief said Elijah would return at the end of history (Mal. 4:5) or that some other prophet would be present to lead the people (Deut. 18:15). Again John uttered denials. "Then who are you?" pressed his questioners. The answer was appropriately modest: "I am a mere voice in the wilderness, crying, 'Make a straight road for the Lord'" (v. 23, P). John was citing a prophecy in Isaiah 40:3. The image was not uncommon in ancient times—kings and emperors often sent slaves in advance to secure the road on which they would travel.

There was only one question left to ask: "Then why are you baptizing at all, if you are not Christ or Elijah or the prophet?" (v. 25, P) That is, if John was not the one officially inaugurating the end of all things, what could be the significance of his baptizing?

John did not hesitate. "I baptize with water," he said. "But among you, in your very midst, stands one unknown to you who will come with another kind of baptism. And I am not worthy to loosen the thong of his sandal" (vv. 26–27, P).

The implication is that Jesus was among those standing on the river bank as John was baptizing. What drama there was in John's words! The real messiah was there, mingling with the crowd of onlookers, and they didn't know who he was.

There was a rabbinical saying at the time that a disciple might perform for his teacher any duty a slave might do for his master except one. He could not loosen his teacher's sandals. The Gospel was explicit: John saw himself as a disciple of Jesus!

O Lord, I, who am not even as worthy as John, beg to be your disciple. Grant that I may never get in your way, so that people see me when they should be seeing you. Baptize me in your Holy Spirit, I pray, that all my thoughts and deeds may glorify you, this day and forever. Amen.

Week 1: Tuesday

John 1:29–34   The Witness of the Spirit

Mark 1:9, Matthew 3:13, and Luke 3:21–22 all represent Jesus as receiving John's baptism. The account in the Fourth Gospel, however, tactfully avoids any scene in which Jesus is baptized. The author has been trying to emphasize John the Baptist's secondary role, and surely sees no point in confusing the issue by referring to the baptism.

Besides, the Christ of this Gospel is too exalted to receive baptism at John's hands. He is the pre-existent Word (1:1–3, 30). He and the Father are one (17:11, 20–23). When he prays, it is not for strength but to let the people know his relationship to the Father (11:42). He does not suffer in Gethsemane as the Jesus of the

Synoptic Gospels does. He is the transcendent Christ, the ruler of the cosmos; it would not be appropriate for John to baptize him.

In the Synoptic tradition, John recognized Jesus as the messiah after the baptism, when the Spirit descended on him like a dove (Mark 1:10; Matt. 3:16; Luke 3:22). Here, John purports to have witnessed the Spirit, but does not link it to Jesus' having been baptized. Apparently the descent occurred at some past time, so that John knew Jesus' real identity when the priests and Levites from Jerusalem came to see him.

It is not clear whether the priests and Levites are still present on this second day when John makes his pronouncements about Jesus; but this does not really matter, for they have served their purpose in the drama by permitting John to clarify his relationship to Jesus.

John makes three statements about Jesus: (1) Jesus is the Lamb of God, who takes away the sin of the world; (2) even though Jesus comes later than John, he existed before John and ranks above him; (3) the Spirit has descended on Jesus, and he is the one who baptizes with the Holy Spirit.

What is meant by the phrase "the Lamb of God"? Some scholars believe it refers to the apocalyptic lamb spoken of in Revelation 7:17 and 17:14, which is an object of terror and will destroy evil in the world. Others see it as the Suffering Servant of Isaiah 52–53, who gives his life for the people of God, or as the paschal lamb, whose blood was smeared on the door posts of the Israelites to save their children from the death-angel (Exod. 12:22). The latter interpretation fits especially well with the sacramentalism of the Fourth Gospel, which has Jesus condemned to death at noon on the day before Passover (19:14), the very hour when the priests began to slay the paschal lambs in the temple. But all of the interpretations are fitting, and it is possible that the author, with his great literary imagination, used the phrase for precisely this reason.

O Lamb of God, I worship you. I praise your name for this rich image of your saving power, and for the Holy Spirit with which you baptize your true followers. Help me to witness faithfully to your coming in my life, as John the Baptist witnessed to your coming in his. For you are indeed the Son of God. Amen.

Week 1: Wednesday

John 1:35–42 A Transference of Disciples

The Gospel presents three days in the life of John the Baptist. On the first, John witnesses to the priests and Levites from Jerusalem (1:19–28). On the second, he points to Jesus as the Lamb of God who takes away the sin of the world (1:29–34). On the third, John again calls Jesus the Lamb of God; and, this time, two disciples who hear John's witness leave John to follow Jesus.

This is the only Gospel that represents any of Jesus' disciples as having originally been disciples of John the Baptist. The other Gospels depict the calling of Andrew, Simon, James, and John at the seashore in Galilee. Many scholars are inclined to believe John's version is more accurate, or that the calling in Galilee occurred after the one in Judea, and the disciples had gone home to fish for a while. This would explain the apparent abruptness of the calling in the Synoptics.

In the case of one of the disciples who left John to follow Jesus, we are not told his name. Speculation suggests it may be John, the beloved disciple, who is mentioned again in 13:23, 19:26, and 21:20.

The scene is quiet but powerful. The two disciples walk away from John and follow Jesus. Jesus looks back, sees them, and asks, "What are you looking for?" It is a question he might ask any of us. The disciples reply by calling him "rabbi," which means "my great one" or "teacher." It is a title the author of the Fourth Gospel is fond of, for it accords well with the emphasis in the prologue on Jesus as the Wisdom of God. The disciples ask where Jesus is staying. He says, "Come and see." They come, and end by staying the entire day with him, because it is "about the tenth hour."

There is uncertainty about whether John's Gospel reckons time from midnight or 6:00 A.M. Probably it is from 6:00 A.M., making the hour 4:00 P.M. This means that the sabbath was upon them and they were unable to travel any distance before the next sunset.

The first thing Andrew does when he leaves Jesus is to go to his brother Simon and tell him they have found the messiah. Simon is to figure much more prominently in the early Christian movement than Andrew, but Simon might not have met Jesus at all if it had not been for Andrew. "We have found the Messiah" could be the most important message ever spoken by a disciple of Jesus, whether in their age or ours.

Jesus changes Simon's name to Cephas (Aramaic *Kēphâ*), which in Greek is *Petros*. The word means "rock," and probably expresses something Jesus sees in Simon's character or physique. In Matthew 16:18 Jesus infers that he calls Simon "rock" because he intends to build his church on him. The Fourth Gospel does not explain the renaming, but we recall that an act of renaming in the Old Testament (e.g., Abram to Abraham or Jacob to Israel) presaged some mighty use of the person renamed.

> O God of Abraham and Israel, of Andrew and Simon Peter, what would you like to call me? What name might evoke the gift I am able to give you? Teach it to me as I pray, and let us have it between us as our secret, that I may hear you when you call me in the night, and respond, "Here am I, Lord." Through Jesus, my great one. Amen.

Week 1: Thursday

John 1:43–51 A Puzzling Disciple

There is something odd about this passage—none of the other Gospels mentions Nathanael as a disciple of Jesus. His name does not appear in the lists of disciples in Matthew 10:1–4, Mark 3:13–19, and Luke 6:12–16. John mentions it again in 21:2, with the information that Nathanael lived in Cana of Galilee. But otherwise he is a man of mystery!

The name *Nathanael* means "God has given." This has led some scholars to speculate that it is another name for Matthew, which means "gift of Yahweh." Others think he is to be identified with Bartholomew, for Bartholomew's name normally follows Philip's in listings of the disciples. Still others link him with Simon the Cananean, wrongly deducing that to be from Cana is to be a Cananean. The early church Fathers concluded that Nathanael did not become one of the Twelve, and so was never listed among them.

Given the custom of having two names, it is possible that Nathanael may have been included in the Synoptic lists under another name. We simply don't know. What is important in this

[23

vignette, however, is not whether Nathanael became one of the Twelve but the exchange he had with Jesus.

As Andrew had found his brother Simon and brought him to Jesus, Philip told his friend Nathanael he had met the one of whom Moses and the prophets had spoken. His name was Jesus. He was the son of Joseph of Nazareth. Nathanael's reaction was a jest, possibly because he came from the same region: "Can anything good come out of Nazareth?" (v. 46) Philip's words were the same ones Jesus had spoken to Andrew and the other disciple first called: "Come and see."

As Nathanael approached, Jesus said, "Behold a true Israelite, one without any guile" (v. 47, P). "How do you know me?" asked Nathanael. "Before Philip called you," answered Jesus, "when you were under the fig tree, I saw you" (v. 48).

On the surface, this is a light-hearted exchange. But John often packs even the simplest scene with deep significance. Nathanael probably represents the *real* Israel, that responds to God's redemptive activity without malice or deviousness. We recall that John was writing especially for Jewish Christians who were being tempted to revert to Judaism; they would have recognized the import of Jesus' hailing Nathanael as "a true Israelite," implying a contrast with the Jews who did not come to Jesus to see whether he was the messiah. The fig tree too is significant. In the Old Testament, the fig tree was often a symbol of a prosperous Israel. Jesus' remark about "a true Israelite" may have been prompted by his seeing Nathanael beneath a fig tree; or, on the other hand, the reference to a fig tree may have been designed to underscore the kind of Israelite Nathanael would become as a result of his coming to Jesus!

Nathanael's response was beautiful. First, he addressed Jesus as rabbi or teacher. Then he called him Son of God. And finally he named him King of Israel, which involves a play on the fact that Jesus had called Nathanael "a true Israelite." The order of progression from rabbi to Son of God to King of Israel is not anticlimactic, as it first appears, but climactic. When Nathanael called Jesus Son of God, it was more than calling him rabbi. And when he called him King of Israel it was more than a theological confession, it was a personal commitment. It was tantamount to saying, "You will be Son of God in *my* life, King of *this* Israelite."

Jesus' response to Nathanael was to tell him that the best was yet to come. If Nathanael had believed on the basis of their simple encounter, his heart would swell at all he would behold in months to come. What he would see would be utterly convincing—as if angels danced from heaven to earth and back again above the head of this man he had taken as his king!

O God, this is an inspiring passage. Help me to take Jesus as my king, that I too may be "a true Israelite." And, as I pray and meditate in the weeks ahead, let me "see" with spiritual eyes this confirming vision of Christ with the angels dancing above his head. For yours is the kingdom and the power and the glory forever. Amen.

Week 1: Friday

John 2:1–12   The Best Wine of All

Once more we are into material not represented in any other Gospel. This is extraordinary when we consider that John says it is the first miracle or sign performed by Jesus. Surely the disciples would never forget such a miracle, and it would figure prominently in all the traditions of the early church. The question naturally arises, did John see significance in this miracle that the other Gospel authors did not see, or was he imagining a story in order to illustrate a truth?

The beginning of the story makes us suspicious: "On the third day there was a marriage." On the third day from what? The answer is not clear. Some exegetes think it is the third day after Jesus' appearance at the place where John the Baptist was baptizing (1:29–34); others, that it is the third day after the calling of Philip and Nathanael (1:43–51). It has even been suggested that the third day is a reference to the resurrection, which occurred on the third day after Jesus' death. If this is true, then the mention of the third day is intended to signal a "spiritual" message to follow, having to do with a quality of life brought about by Jesus' resurrection. The possibility that this interpretation may be correct is enhanced by the fact that Jesus refers in verse 4 to his "hour"—a usage which in John always alludes to the hour of crucifixion and glorification (cf. 7:30, 8:20, 12:23, 12:27, 13:1, 17:1).

An Eastern wedding was a joyous occasion, often lasting seven days. It began with the friends of the bridegroom escorting the bride to the home of the groom, where there would be a great wedding feast. Friends and family members came from miles away. As Cana was only a few miles from Nazareth (some geographers identify it with a village two miles away, others with a village nine miles away), it is probable that Jesus' mother was related to the bride or the groom. At any rate, she and Jesus and his disciples came—including, presumably, Nathanael, whose home was in Cana.

At some point in the festivities—possibly after three or four days—the wine ran out. Jesus' mother came to him and said, "They have no wine." Jesus said, literally, "What is it to me and you, woman? For it is not yet my hour" (v. 4). The part played by Jesus' mother in urging him to perform the miracle has led some interpreters to believe that she felt responsible for the shortage. The wine at most weddings was furnished by the guests. Perhaps Jesus and his friends came with his mother, bringing no extra wine, and their presence caused the supply to give out.

It is doubtless significant that the miracle involved six stone jars that held water for the Jewish rites of purification. The number six meant incompleteness to the Jews, as the number seven meant completeness. If we assume that the wine had sacramental meaning—as a symbol of the Christian Eucharist or communion—we see the contrast between the inadequacy of the old religion and the fullness of the new. The steward of the feast—probably a friend of the bridegroom—pronounced the new wine even better than the wine they had already had, though it was customary to have the best wine served first at a feast.

In verse 11, John says this was the first of Jesus' signs (there will be many more in the Gospel) that "manifested his glory." "Glory" is a special word in the Gospel, and is usually related to the hour of Jesus' death. In the crucifixion, he will be lifted up for all to see (3:14) and the Father will glorify him (17:1).

Each of us must decide individually whether the author of the Gospel intended the story literally or symbolically. But, either way, it is impossible to miss a certain symbolic level in the passage. Early Christians could hardly have heard the account read in their presence without finding eucharistic meaning in it. Jesus is the one who gives the new wine of the kingdom. Wedding feasts were often used as a sign of the eschatological banquet—the great ingathering of God at the end of time. And Nathanael, the true Israelite (1:43–51), must surely have seen this.

O Lord, the old wine of my life has failed me. I thirst for the new wine of your presence and power. Come into my daily affairs, I pray, and give me a banqueting spirit. Transform the inadequate forms of religion in my life into wellsprings of faith and joy. For your wine is above all wines, and your kingdom beyond compare. Amen.

Week 1: Saturday

John 2:13–22 Talking about Temples

In the Synoptic Gospels, this scene occurs during the final days of Jesus' ministry and is instrumental in provoking the scribes and Pharisees to seek his death (Matt. 21:12–17; Mark 11:15–19; Luke 19:45–48). In John, Jesus visits Jerusalem not once but many times, and the cleansing of the temple comes at the beginning of his public ministry.

There may be significance in the placement of the story near the account of the wedding in Cana. At the wedding feast, Jesus demonstrated the superiority of the new order over the old. Here he moves from talking about the old temple to speaking of the new temple of his body, which would be raised up in three days.

We remember that the Gospel was written to encourage Christian Jews not to return to Judaism in order to continue worshiping in the synagogues. This passage had obvious meaning for such persons, because, in effect, it relocated "holy space" for them. Sacred space was no longer in a temple or in synagogues; Jesus had transcended all of this in his death and resurrection.

The cleansing of the temple precincts—the outer courts where birds and animals were sold and currencies were exchanged—became a mere launching point for the conversation with "the Jews," which is the weightier part of the passage. Those who sold birds and animals for sacrifices represented the old order of atonement, which the Epistle to the Hebrews would declare to be superseded by Jesus. Those exchanging money did so because the temple tax of half a shekel could not be paid in Greek or Roman coinage, which bore the images of pagan gods and emperors; they simply traded acceptable Tyrian coins for the other money, making a profit on each exchange. By fashioning a whip, probably from the rushes used to bed down the animals, and driving out the sellers and exchangers, Jesus was establishing himself in the tradition of the prophet Jeremiah. Jeremiah cried, "Has this house, which is called by my name, become a den of robbers in your eyes?" (Jer.

7:11), and threatened that God would destroy the temple in Jerusalem as he had the one in Shiloh.

The quotation "Zeal for thy house will consume me" is from Psalm 69. The context of the citation is interesting:

> I have become a stranger to my brethren,
>   an alien to my mother's sons.
> For zeal for thy house has consumed me,
>   and the insults of those who insult thee
>   have fallen on me (vv. 8–9).

Taken alone, the phrase would indicate that Jesus did what he did because he was overwhelmed by feeling for the house of God. In its fuller context, the saying has another meaning—that his concern for the purity of the old religion, represented by the temple, has led to his disfavor among others, so that he receives the insults of those who were by their behavior insulting God.

In the conflict with "the Jews" (the Synoptics speak of chief priests, scribes, and elders), Jesus spoke with a double meaning. They asked for a sign of his authority—a miracle to attest to his messiahship. He answered with a dare: "Destroy this temple, and in three days I will raise it up" (v. 19). They assumed he referred to the temple from whose grounds he had driven the sellers and money-changers. In fact, he was referring to his own body.

Again there is a possible connection to the passage about the wedding feast at Cana. It too took place "on the third day" and was suggestive of the fullness of life to come through Jesus' resurrection.

It is little wonder, when Jesus had been raised from the dead, that his disciples remembered all these things and reconsidered them in the context of resurrection-faith. Then such incidents made sense to them in new and dynamic ways.

Lord, the old temple of my life is cluttered with things that dishonor you. Come in your cleansing presence, I pray, and drive them out. Resacralize my heart as a dwelling place for your Holy Spirit, and I shall praise you in word and deed, for yours is the glory forever. Amen.

WEEK 2

Week 2: Sunday

John 2:23–25 A Wary Jesus

The Gospel of John emphasizes a few signs or miracles of Jesus to the exclusion of many others described in the Synoptic Gospels. Here the others are at least mentioned. But we also receive an insight into the importance of the signs in John. They are significant for their spiritual teachings, not as proofs of Jesus' authority. Jesus himself disdains those who believe in him merely because they have seen some unusual act of power. This fits well with the saying in 20:29, "Blessed are those who have not seen and yet believe." The premium is on understanding, not on excitation by signs and miracles.

Verses 24–25 are a sad note on human nature. Jesus knew better than to trust the applause of the crowd, because he "knew what was in man." He understood the fickleness and selfishness of which we are all capable, and he knew it could rise in an instant at the least provocation. The very people who would shout "Hosanna" as he rode into Jerusalem would be crying for his crucifixion only a few days later.

Against the ephemeral nature of popular approval, we can better evaluate the devotion of the few disciples who remained faithful to Jesus through his ministry, trial, and death. They clung to him not because of what they had seen but because of what they understood about the coming of a new order. This is why John so preferred the title of rabbi for Jesus—he taught the disciples understanding.

If I understand why Jesus was wary of popular acclaim, Lord, it is because I know the fickleness of my own heart. Like the people of Jerusalem, I am inclined to be more excited about outward signs than inner meanings. Teach me to be quiet and to study hidden connections, that I may be faithful in all things. Through Jesus the Christ. Amen.

Week 2: Monday

John 3:1–12   A Teacher of Spiritual Things

There was drama in this brief encounter. It occurred at night. It was between Jesus and a member of the Sanhedrin, the seventy ruling elders of Israel. And it pitted one teacher against another—a wonder-working newcomer against an established interpreter of the Law.

Nicodemus came to Jesus at night. Perhaps he did not wish to be seen in the company of the rabbi from Galilee; or maybe he chose that time because Jewish elders enjoyed discussing the Law at night. But we must not overlook the symbolism of light and darkness in John. When John describes the scene in which Jesus confronted Judas about betraying him, he concludes by saying that Judas went out into the night (13:30). Jesus is the light of the world (8:12), and those who are not with him are children of darkness.

Nicodemus began the conversation respectfully. It was obvious, he said, that Jesus had God's authority behind him—else he could not have done the wonders he had been doing. Jesus' answer, though, was not about wonders but about the kingdom of God. A truly spiritual teacher, he implied, one born from above, would have recognized that that was what he was about.

The Greek word *anōthen* means both "again" and "above." It has often been interpreted in the sense of "again" by those who use the phrase "born again." But that is the way Nicodemus misinterpreted it, so that he asked, "How can a man be born when he is old? Can he enter a second time into his mother's womb and be born?" (v. 4) Jesus' remark in verse 5, that one must be born "of water and the Spirit," reflects his real intention in the word: to participate in the kingdom of God, one must be born (or receive *begottenness)* from above, from the world of the Spirit.

"It is like the wind," said Jesus, making another word-play (the Greek word *pneuma* means both "wind" and "Spirit"). "It blows where it wishes, and you hear its voice, but you don't know where it comes from or where it is going" (v. 8, P).

In other words, the Spirit world is a mystery too deep for mere human teachers to understand. Nicodemus may have been an expert in the Law, but even a natural force like the wind was beyond his powers of explanation. How could he hope to understand the kingdom of God? And, if he did not know what to make of Jesus' teachings up to this point, how could he possibly comprehend the deeper spiritual truths Jesus was capable of imparting?

We should consider the effect of this story on John's audience of Christian Jews. Nicodemus was one of the most learned men of Israel—one of the great teachers—and he appeared as a mere school child in the presence of the Master. Why would any Christian choose to return to Judaism, forsaking such a teacher as Jesus? Nathanael was clearly a wiser Jew than Nicodemus; he not only called Jesus Teacher, he also called him Son of God and King of Israel (1:49). No wonder Jesus called Nathanael, not Nicodemus, "a true Israelite." It was through him, and others like him, that the kingdom of God would be realized.

Nicodemus will make two later appearances in the Gospel. In 7:50–51, he will try to restrain the Pharisees in their immoderate attempt to silence Jesus. And in 19:38–42, he will come with Joseph of Arimathea, carrying a great mixture of burial ointment, to prepare the body of Jesus for entombment. The effect of these two references is to assure us that Nicodemus became a crypto-disciple, a secret follower of Jesus. But there is something sad about the stealthiness of his discipleship. It suggests that those who have most to lose are least likely to identify themselves wholeheartedly with Jesus. Being born from above is not as easy for them as for the simple folk like Simon and Nathanael. Their risk is greater, and they are inclined to approach Jesus more cautiously.

O God, it frightens me that I may know many things, as Nicodemus did, and still miss the truths of the Spirit. Teach me to be open to your presence, that I may discern what you are doing in my world and worship you. Through Jesus your Son. Amen.

Week 2: Tuesday

John 3:13–21   A Word from the Author

These verses have traditionally been treated as part of Jesus' words to Nicodemus. It is entirely possible, however, that they are a gloss by the author himself—a short sermon prompted by Jesus' encounter with the Jewish ruler. Ancient manuscripts employed no quotation marks or paragraph indentations to guide us in making such determinations; we must simply judge by the words themselves.

Verse 13, "No one has ascended into heaven but he who descended from heaven, the Son of man," makes little sense if spoken by Jesus. The Latin manuscripts and some Greek manuscripts of the Gospel add to the end of the sentence the words "who is in heaven." This, as well as the verses to follow, seems fitting if the speaker is not Jesus but rather the author of the Gospel.

When the Israelites were in the wilderness, they complained of the lack of food and water. God sent a plague of serpents among them, and many persons died. When the people repented, Moses prayed for them. God instructed Moses to make a brazen serpent and set it on a pole for bearing standards; anyone who looked at it would live (Num. 21:4–9).

Now John picks up this ancient image and applies it to Jesus' being lifted up. As it was a serpent that saved the people from the bites of serpents, it is a human being, the incarnate Word, who will save people from themselves and the human situation. The word for "pole" in Numbers 21:9 is also the word for "sign," and this was surely in John's mind. The real sign that Jesus gives, finally, is his being lifted up, both in his crucifixion and in his ascension. And anyone who regards this sign faithfully will have not only life but *eternal* life.

John is the Gospel of eternal life. Again and again this theme predominates. The phrase means more than everlasting life, though that is part of it. Understood cumulatively throughout the

32]

Gospel, it signifies a special quality of life—an unusual nature conferred on those who are born from above, not by the will of the flesh but by the will of God.

God loved the world, says John; he sent his only begotten Son into the world so that the world could be saved. The emphasis is not on the *whole* world, as one sometimes hears in sermons, but on the world as the opposite of the Spirit. We are back at the Wisdom theme of 1:1–18—Jesus has come as the light of the world in order to save us from darkness.

The people who have seen the great sign—Jesus' being lifted up and received back into the bosom of the Father—have escaped the condemnation of the darkness. Those who have not accepted the sign—presumably the Jewish leaders—are condemned for loving the darkness more than the light.

O God of brightness and glory, I tremble to think how I am inclined to darkness and shadow in my life. My spirit is lazy and my deeds are often selfish. Forgive me, I pray, and teach me to love the light who has come into the world. For he has been lifted up and set above all darkness forever and ever. Amen.

Week 2: Wednesday

John 3:22–30   The Friend of the Bridegroom

When we think of joy, it is usually in terms of growing or expanding—of having more friends, receiving more acclaim, making more money. In this passage we encounter a contrary phenomenon. John the Baptist says that his joy is most complete at the moment when Christ's popularity must increase and his own decrease.

John and his disciples were baptizing at Aenon, probably a settlement along the Jordan River (the location is uncertain today), when a certain Jew engaged the disciples in conversation about purification rites. The Gospel does not tell us which rites were in question. Probably the discussion was related to some difference between what John taught about baptism and what Jesus taught about it. (We know from Mark 2:18–22 that people questioned the differences between John's and Jesus' teachings about fasting; and the same metaphor, of the bridegroom, figures strongly in that passage.)

The disciples, possibly with new information obtained from the Jew, came to John in a state of disturbance. The crowds were leaving John and going to Jesus, they reported.

John's reply was calm and confident. It had two parts.

First, Jesus was receiving the people because God had given them to him. This is a consistent theme in John's Gospel (6:39, 10:29, 17:2, 9, 11, 24). God is sovereign, and all those he gives to Jesus must come to him; conversely, any who are not given may not come.

Second, Jesus was the bridegroom of the kingdom and John was only the friend of the bridegroom. It was the friend's job, in Jewish culture, to prepare the wedding feast and have everything in readiness for the nuptials. It would have been the grossest impropriety for the friend of the groom to have tried in any way to take the groom's place with the bride. Instead, the friend waited with the bride until other friends of the groom came and brought her to the groom. Then the friend rejoiced to hear the sound of the groom's voice, and turned his charge over to the groom. At that moment, the groom became everything to the bride, and it was time for the friend to fade away. Therefore John said, "He must increase, but I must decrease" (v. 30).

The author may have included this remarkable passage to remind disciples of John the Baptist that John deferred to Jesus and surrendered his ministry to him. But it is also an effective reminder to us about our own places in the kingdom. We worry more than we should about being recognized for our contributions to Christ's ministry in the world. But Christ is the bridegroom and we are only his friends; it is appropriate for us to do our duty and then retire from the limelight. The real focus of spiritual joy is on Christ and his church.

Thank you, God, for this beautiful picture of the relationship between Jesus and John. Help me too to be a friend of the groom and do everything I can for his bride. In his glorious name. Amen.

Week 2: Thursday

John 3:31–36   The Witness from Above

This is another of John's editorial comments. Just as he followed the account of Nicodemus' visit with the short sermon about Jesus (3:13–21), now he follows the story of John's waning popularity with a brief homily.

"He who comes from above is above all," says John. The emphasis is similar to that in Jesus' words to Nicodemus, that one must be born *from above* to see the kingdom (3:3). Jesus is above all earthly teachers—John the Baptist as well as Nicodemus—and whoever accepts his teachings has eternal life.

Verses 32–33 appear to contain contradictory statements. First we read, "no one receives his testimony," and then we see, "he who receives his testimony sets his seal to this, that God is true." Apparently the first statement is hyperbolic—an exaggeration. "Practically *nobody* is paying attention to Jesus' teachings. But"—and this gives force to the second statement—"any who *do* pay attention are receiving life from above."

The Jerusalem Bible translates the passage in a way to resolve the difficulty:

> He who comes from heaven
> bears witness to the things he has seen and heard,
> even if his testimony is not accepted;
> though all who do accept his testimony
> are attesting the truthfulness of God (31–33).

It is interesting that John gives this insight into the popularity of the faith. Several times in the Gospel we receive the impression that great crowds flocked about Jesus. Perhaps this remark indicates a feeling of depression experienced by many Christians through the ages because so few persons, considering the size of the population, have responded to the light.

Verse 36 is a statement parallel to verse 18—whoever believes in the Son has eternal life, but whoever does not is already experiencing the wrath of God. In the Synoptic Gospels, the wrath of God was spoken of as occurring in the future. In John, it is already operative, just as eternal life is a quality of being in believers' lives now, not only in the life beyond death.

Lord, I am concerned about all the people who are even now experiencing your wrath. How terrible it must be to live from day to day with darkness and hopelessness. I pray for your grace in their lives, that somehow they may turn to the light and find a new quality of being. Through Jesus Christ. Amen.

Week 2: Friday

John 4:1–15   A Greater than Jacob

This is the beginning of a longer story with several interesting highlights. You may wish to read the entire narrative, verses 1–42, on each of three successive days while we are examining sections of it. There are so many things to notice that each reading will prove richer and more interesting than the last.

We are told that Jesus "had to pass through Samaria" (v. 4). Geographically this was not true, especially if Jesus and the disciples had been baptizing in the Jordan River; they could have followed the valley north into Galilee. But perhaps John was speaking of another kind of constraint—the spiritual necessity that appears to have governed Jesus throughout the Gospel. In other words, the meeting with the woman at the well could have been more than a coincidence; it may have been divine destiny.

It was noontime, and Jesus was tired. He had probably been traveling since daybreak or before. In good rabbinical fashion, he sat by a wayside well to rest while his disciples went into town to purchase food. The town was called Sychar, apparently the settlement known in modern times as Shechem, directly on the north-south route between Jerusalem and Galilee.

Noon was an odd time for the woman to be coming for water. Water for household uses was normally drawn early in the morning or late in the day. We know, however, that the woman had a loose reputation. Perhaps she came at an hour when she expected to encounter no one in the vicinity of the well. It is true that we often meet God's messengers when we least expect them.

Jesus violated tradition by asking the woman for a drink. She was a Samaritan, and there had been ill will between Jews and Samaritans for centuries. Jews considered the Samaritans half-breeds, as the Jews who had once lived in Samaria were systematically intermarried with Babylonians and Medes after the fall of the Northern Kingdom in 722 B.C. The average Jew would have deemed a Samaritan's cooking utensils or drinking vessels unclean—ritually impure for eating or drinking—and Jesus asked to drink from the woman's water jar. But the biggest scandal of all, as evidenced by the disciples' amazement in verse 27, was that Jesus should speak publicly to a woman, whatever her race. Most men of that day would not address even their own wives in a public place, much less a strange woman like this.

Like the authors of the other Gospels, John apparently viewed Jesus' behavior as an evidence of his messiahship. The Lord of creation transcended the parochial rules by which other men lived.

"If you knew the gift of God," said Jesus when the woman did not immediately give him the drink he requested, "and who it is that is saying to you, 'Give me a drink,' you would have asked him and he would have given you living water" (v. 10). "The gift of God" probably means "the Spirit of God" or "the Spirit of truth," which in the Johannine literature is always treated as a divine gift. Had the woman only been aware that the final age had come and that she was standing in the presence of the Lord of that age, she would have been seeking the water of life from him.

As is typical in John, what Jesus is saying is misunderstood (cf. the interview with Nicodemus in 3:1–12). The woman's reply in verse 11, about his having nothing to draw with, indicates that she has taken his words "living water" to mean mere "running water" or "flowing water," not the water of eternal life. Is he greater than their common ancestor Jacob, she asks, who discovered the well where she draws water? Even for Jacob it was not a place of running water, but a *phrear*, a mere cistern, from which water had always been drawn by hand.

Jesus' reply underscores the difference between the Old Order and the New: "Every one who drinks of this water will thirst again, but whoever drinks of the water that I shall give him will never thirst; the water that I shall give him will become in him a spring of water welling up to eternal life" (vv. 13–14). The Greek word for "welling up" (*hallesthai*) means "leaping or springing up" and implies great liveliness and activity. What a declaration this must have been to Christian Jews who were tempted to forsake their Christianity in order to return to the synagogues. The faith that had come to them through Jacob and the patriarchs would leave them always thirsting for more; what had come to them in Jesus was fully satisfying, and would be so forever.

Again typically, the woman didn't understand. She thought they were still talking about mere physical water. But she was so impressed by the words of the stranger that she asked him for the water that would end her trips to the well.

Is there a reference to Christian baptism in this passage about "living water"? Interpreters disagree. But it is hard to believe that John, who was extraordinarily sensitive to the meaning of words and symbols, would not have reflected on the relationship between the "spring of water welling up to eternal life" and the words Jesus had spoken only shortly before to Nicodemus: "Truly, truly, I say to you, unless one is born of water and the Spirit, he cannot enter the kingdom of God" (3:5).

God, I am as guilty as "the Jews" of forgetting how far above tradition Jesus is—how much nearer the center of your being, how much wiser, and how much more compassionate. Let me now, in the quietness of my meditation, experience his transcendent glory, that my life may be transformed by his presence. For his name's sake. Amen.

Week 2: Saturday

John 4:16–26   The Meaning of True Worship

We recall that the woman at the well, beginning to believe the words of Jesus but still not fully understanding them, asked him to give her the water that would quench her thirst for all time (v. 15). Jesus' response was to tell her to go and bring her husband.

The woman said she had no husband. Jesus said she had spoken truly, for she had had five husbands and was presently living with a man who was not her husband. John may have been using words with double meanings again, as he did in the exchange between Jesus and Nicodemus. The Hebrew word for husband was *ba'al*, which was also the popular word for deity. When Jesus said that the woman had had five husbands, he might also have been saying she had had five gods, and that the god she now worshiped was not her god at all.

Supposing that the conversation was only about husbands, however, we see something of the woman's moral character and how truly unsatisfying her religious faith had been in her personal life. The law forbade Jewish women to marry more than three times. Although the woman was a Samaritan, she had obviously married more often than women generally did.

Jesus exhibited the kind of insight into the woman's affairs that he had shown with Nathanael (1:45–51) and Nicodemus (3:1–12). As John said in 2:25, he "knew what was in man." His extraordinary power of perception led the woman to guess that he was a prophet, and she initiated a conversation about worship.

The Samaritans had always worshiped on Mount Gerizim, at whose base stood the town of Sychar and Jacob's well. There had even been a temple on the mountain until a Maccabean king, John Hyrcanus, destroyed it about a century before Jesus. Orthodox Jewish worship, on the other hand, had long been centralized in Jerusalem. Jews worshiped in synagogues, but the temple was considered the absolute focus of their worship.

The woman alluded to the fact of religious pluralism: people had different ideas about where they should worship. But Jesus used her words as a springboard for the most important truth of these few verses—that the hour was now at hand when worship at all holy places was superseded by a new kind of worship. "God is spirit," he said, "and those who worship him must worship in spirit and truth" (v. 24).

This was precisely the message needed by Christians being forced out of synagogue worship—that the time had come when God's rule was everywhere and there was no more requirement for sacred locations. The coming of the kingdom had rendered the old dependence on holy places null and void.

The woman's understanding was growing, as Nathanael's had. Did she dare hope that Jesus was the messiah—the one called Taheb in her religion? "I know that Messiah is coming," she said; "when he comes, he will show us all things" (v. 25). "I who speak to you," said Jesus, "am he" (v. 26).

Egō eimi are the Greek words—"I am." It is a phrase we shall meet again and again in John. "I am the bread of life" (6:35). "I am the light of the world" (8:12). "I am the door of the sheep" (10:7, 9). "I am the beautiful shepherd" (10:11, 14, P). "I am the resurrection and the life" (11:25). "I am the way, and the truth, and the life" (14:6). "I am the vine" (15:1, 5). Used alone as in this passage, without any modifier, the words I AM carry a definitive, regal impact—as when God said to Moses, when Moses asked his name, "I AM WHO I AM" (Exod. 3:14).

The one speaking to the woman at the well was the eternal Word, present at the creation of the world!

Lord, it often seems easy to worship you in church, where everything reminds me to look for your presence. Teach me, I pray, to expect you everywhere; for every place is holy if you are there, and there is no place where you may not be found. Amen.

WEEK 3

Week 3: Sunday

John 4:27–42   The Beginning of the Harvest

When the woman saw the disciples returning, she left her water
jar and ran into the city to tell the people about the extraordinary
stranger she had met. Why did she go so abruptly? Perhaps because
the appearance of the disciples convinced her that Jesus was a
special person; or because she knew they would not approve of her
talking with their Master. Some interpreters have seen in the
forsaken water jar a symbol of her inadequate religion, similar to
the symbolic meaning of the six stone jars at the wedding feast in
Cana (2:6). For the moment, at least, she had lost all interest in
water from the well of Jacob; she had discovered the one who could
give her "living water."

"Come," the woman exclaimed to the townspeople, "see a man
who told me all that I ever did. Can this be the Christ?" (v. 29)

Had Jesus indeed told her everything? If so, we have received
only fragments of the conversation. Considering the time required
for the disciples to purchase food, we can imagine a much more
extensive interchange. Jesus apparently touched the deepest feelings of the woman, causing her to become excited and voluble
about the experience.

Meanwhile, the disciples set food in front of Jesus and were worried that he didn't eat. "Rabbi, eat," they said. But Jesus said, in effect, that he was feeding on something else. He was beholding the coming of the kingdom, and the vision nourished him.

Others had sown the seeds of the kingdom. Now he and the disciples were reaping the harvest. They had entered fields prepared by others, and the disciples' labors would bring them eternal life.

The Samaritan village was among the first fruits of the harvest time. The people entreated Jesus to stay with them, and he remained in their midst for two days. When he left, they said to the woman, "At first we believed because of what you said; now we believe because we have experienced the man himself, and are convinced that he is the Savior of the world" (v. 42, P).

> *Lord, it was this way in my life, too. At first I believed because others spoke of you. Then I experienced your presence for myself. It was like nothing else that has ever happened to me. Grant, dear Master, that the memory of the event may remain strong and fresh in my mind, and that your presence may continue with me always. For your name's sake. Amen.*

Week 3: Monday

John 4:43–54   More Fruits of the Kingdom

Leaving the Samaritan village, Jesus continued his journey into Galilee, where, according to verse 45, he received an enthusiastic welcome. Some Galileans had been in Jerusalem for the Passover and had obviously brought back to their region tales of the signs Jesus had given there. Verse 44, the saying about a prophet's being without honor in his own country, seems out of place here, and logically antithetical to verse 45; many scholars believe it to be the insertion of a redactor who unwisely put it in here because of the mention of Galilee.

Apparently Jesus stayed again in Cana, the home of Nathanael. Perhaps he lodged with the couple at whose wedding feast he had turned water into wine. The references to that sign in verse 46 and to the two signs performed in Galilee, in verse 54, indicate that John saw a special connection between the two stories.

The official whose son was ill in Capernaum, about twenty miles from Cana, was called a *basilikos*, a term meaning "ruler" or "servant of a ruler." If there are parallels of this story in Matthew 8:5–13 and Luke 7:2–10, as some commentators believe, the man was probably a centurion, a Roman officer, for that is what he is in both Synoptic accounts. In those accounts, however, it was a servant or a slave who lay ill, not a son; John's account is more intensely personal than theirs.

The man may have heard reports of Jesus' powers all the way from Jerusalem. We can imagine his hesitance, if he was a Roman, to come to a Jewish rabbi for help. But his son lay dying, and his compassion for the boy overcame any reluctance. He came to Jesus and begged for help. Jesus' reply appears tinged with rebuke, recalling his reaction in Mark 7:27 and Matthew 15:26 to the Syrophoenician woman who asked a miracle for her sick daughter. Putting the kindest interpretation on it, it is a momentary demurring lest people fasten upon "signs and wonders" and not receive the truth of the kingdom lying behind them. But the man importuned Jesus. "Sir," he said, "come down before my child dies" (v. 49). The Greek word *kurios* means both "sir" and "lord." It is possible that the man had moved to a deeper level of respect and expectation, and that this indication of faith in the kingdom, as well as compassion for the dying boy, led Jesus to do as he asked.

"Go," said Jesus; "your son will live."

Content that it was so, the man began his descent from the hills to the seacoast around Capernaum. While he was still on his way, his servants met him with news that his son had survived the crisis. At what hour did he begin to improve, asked the father. At the seventh hour, the servants said—probably an hour past noon. The father remembered, that was the hour when Jesus had said his son would live. "And he himself believed," says John, "and all his household" (v. 53).

There are two significant things about this passage.

First, assuming that the *basilikos* was a centurion, or a Gentile, the passage completes an idea begun in chapter one when Jesus called the disciples and in chapter three when he was visited by Nicodemus. Jesus presented himself first to the Jews, then to the Samaritans (the woman at the well and the people of her village, in 4:1–42), and finally to the Gentiles. This is the model of the gospel's progress as noted in Acts 1:8: "You shall be my witnesses in Jerusalem and in all Judea and Samaria and to the end of the earth." And the conversion of the man's household foreshadows a

[43

pattern found in Acts 10:2, 11:14, 16:15, 31, 34, and 18:8. So the passage is an example of the way Christianity moved out from Jerusalem and Jesus became identified as "the Savior of the world" (John 4:42).

Second, the emphasis of the passage is on *life*, a central theme in John. "In him was life," said the prologue, "and the life was the light of men" (1:4). "Truly, truly, I say to you," Jesus will say in chapter five, "the hour is coming, and now is, when the dead will hear the voice of the Son of God, and those who hear will live" (5:25). This story of the ruler's son forms a transition to a section of the Gospel even more strongly concerned with the subject of life than the one we have been reading.

> *O God, it is so easy for me to confuse mere living with life itself. Like the child's father in this story, I become concerned about survival. Help me to see my own existence more from your perspective than from mine, and to be able to say, "Whether I live or whether I die, I am the Lord's." Then I shall praise you as the Lord of life—eternal life—and never worry about death. For you are the God of the living, not the dead. Amen.*

Week 3: Tuesday

John 5:1–9a   A Healing on the Sabbath

An early Greek tradition identifies the "feast of the Jews" in verse 1 as Pentecost, the Feast of Weeks. There would be a certain appropriateness in this, because Pentecost was the festival celebrating Moses' reception of the Law on Mount Sinai, and the passage to follow (5:2–18) represents Jesus' superiority to the Law in performing a sign on the sabbath.

The sign occurred at the site of an ancient pool near an area where sheep were brought for sacrifice in the temple—hence the reference to the Sheep Gate. The pool and the five marble porticos surrounding it have been excavated in this century, and visitors may descend to the waters by two rather precipitous stairways. It is theorized that the pool is fed by a deep spring that once flowed intermittently, causing the water to roil up as if stirred by an angel. Some old manuscripts contain an extra clause between verses 3 and

4 saying that an angel did indeed stir the waters, and that the first crippled or paralyzed person into the waters after such a visitation was healed of his affliction. While textual evidence for this information is weak, it may nevertheless represent a legend about the pool that actually existed.

We can imagine the scene around the pool on a typical day. There would have been dozens of poor, unfortunate people sitting or lying about on their mats. Most would have shown signs of poverty or squalor. Some would have had twisted limbs. Others would have suffered various degrees of paralysis. For hours at a time, they would have lain there, some waiting quietly, others moaning or talking.

Whenever the waters of the pool began to move, those who lay closest would scream and claw to get in. Relatives or friends waiting nearby would hasten to help their loved ones into the water, hoping to be part of a miracle.

Jesus singled out a man who had lain often by the pool but had never been able to get into the water ahead of the others. The man had been lame for thirty-eight years, and Jesus surely knew his circumstances in the same way he knew all about Nathanael (2:47) and the woman at the well (4:39). Stopping before the man, Jesus looked at him intently. "Rise," he said; "take up your mat, and walk" (v. 8, P).

Immediately the man was healed and did as he was told.

How surprised he must have been to feel life surging in his long-unused limbs! What trembling steps he must have taken, as if he were a baby first learning to walk. And what a wave of shock and excitement must have swept over all those who lay about the old pool.

"Why, we have seen that man here for years," some probably said. "We never thought he would walk again!"

The early church evidently saw a symbolic relationship between this story and Christian baptism, because the scripture, along with the story of Nicodemus in 3:1–21 and that of the blind man in 9:1–40, was one of three Johannine passages used to prepare new Christians for their baptismal rites. Perhaps the story was viewed in the same manner as was the water-into-wine story of 2:1–11, as showing the superiority of Jesus over the old order of Judaism. The man had lain by the pool with five doorways (symbolizing the Pentateuch, or five books of the Law) for thirty-eight years, and Jesus, the Son of the new order, had healed him in a moment!

Lord, my heart swells for what happened to this man by the pool. What power you have to transform the lives of those who were dependent on insufficient forms of religion! Touch the areas of my life that have not responded to you, I pray, and cause them to respond to your glory. For you are the hope of all who have waited a long time. Amen.

Week 3: Wednesday

John 5:9b–18 The Fury of the Jews

How do you feel when something good happens to someone else? Are you delighted in the person's good fortune? Do you feel almost as happy and excited as if it had happened to you?

That is the way it ought to be. Our love and regard for others should enable us to participate in their joy and happiness as if it were our own.

But that is not the way it was with "the Jews" when the lame man was healed by the pool of Bethzatha. Instead of rejoicing in the man's new wholeness as a human being, they became upset and angry because they saw him carrying his little mattress through the streets of Jerusalem. An article in the Mishnah, part of the embellishment on the Law, expressly forbade carrying an empty bed on the sabbath. Caring more for the Law than for the crippled man who was healed, "the Jews" immediately attacked the man for transgressing the sabbath rules.

The man responded to this attack by saying he was only doing what his benefactor had commanded him to do. The man who healed him had told him to take up his pallet and walk away. This simple-minded man was not attempting to fix the blame on Jesus; he was merely describing how he had come to be walking through the streets of Jerusalem with his mat under his arm.

"The Jews" demanded to know the name of the man's benefactor. The man did not know. In his excitement, he had not even bothered to learn the name of the one who had helped him.

Later, Jesus saw the man in the temple, possibly making a sacrifice of thanksgiving for his healing. "Ah, you are all right now," said Jesus. "Take care not to sin, lest something worse befall you" (v. 14, P).

(This last sentence is difficult to interpret, for it is directly opposed to Luke 13:1–5 and John 9:3, in which Jesus refuses to draw a connection between sin and human affliction. Perhaps it was added by a well-meaning scribe who thought this was a good place to inject a little moral lesson for people who are in a healthy condition. On the other hand, the idea of retributive welfare is consistent with sayings in John about children of the light seeking the light because their deeds are good, while others seek the darkness because their deeds are evil [3:19–21, 11:9–10, 12:35–36].)

Having seen Jesus again, the man went to "the Jews" and told them it was Jesus who had healed him. He had no apparent motive for doing this, and seems to have been ignorant of any consequences of the act. Characteristically, in John's Gospel, people do what they have to do in order to fulfill the drama of salvation.

"The Jews" then went to Jesus and raised objections to the sabbath healing. His reply was pointed: God did not stop working on the sabbath; why should he, as the Father's Son? This naturally irritated "the Jews" even more. Not only did Jesus heal on the sabbath, he claimed to be equal with God. John had said in the prologue of the Gospel that Jesus was in the beginning with God and participated in the creation of everything. But this was something "the Jews" could never believe. Therefore a conflict between them and Jesus was inevitable and would lead eventually to Jesus' death.

O Lord, grant that I may never care more about religious rules and practices than I do about any human being. As Jesus transcended all earthly forms and places of worship, so let my spirit rise above all petty and parochial concerns, that you may be glorified in a loving care for all the world. Amen.

Week 3: Thursday

John 5:19–30   The Authority of the Son

These verses continue a discourse obviously begun in verse 17, when Jesus answered "the Jews" after healing a crippled man on the sabbath. They explain in more detail the authority of the Son to heal and give life, as well as to condemn those who refuse to believe in him.

The argument, as C. H. Dodd has pointed out, is essentially from analogy. In primitive Israel, sons learned their fathers' trades; they could literally do only what their fathers did before them. "Truly, truly, I say to you," said Jesus, "the Son can do nothing of his own accord, but only what he sees the Father doing" (v. 19). In other words, if Jesus were not the Son of God, and had not seen God healing on the sabbath, he would have been unable to do it himself.

But Jesus goes further. Not only has he learned to do what the Father did, but now the Father has turned his work over to Jesus, much as an earthly father retires and puts his son in charge of the business. "The Father judges no one, but has given all judgment to the Son, that all may honor the Son, even as they honor the Father" (vv. 22–23).

Judgment here means positive as well as negative judgment—judgment to life as well as to death. God's work is seen principally as the work of judgment—of making decisions about the life or death of men.

Now that Jesus is in charge of the judging, those who hear him and believe his word receive eternal life; those who do not are condemned accordingly. Moreover, this power of Jesus extends not only to the living but to the dead. Even people in their tombs will hear the voice of the Son and come forth to be judged by him. Those who have led good lives will receive "resurrection of life" (*anástasin zōēs*) and those who have done evil will receive "resurrection of judgment" *anástasin kriseōs*). That is, the good will go on living and the bad will have their evil deeds raised against them, and, presumably, return to their torpid states.

The guarantee of the Son's justice lies in the fact that he does none of the judging for himself, according to his own will, but does it all for the Father who sent him. Again, it is the good name of the Father that insures the validity of the Son's work.

> *Teach me, O God, to do your work as Jesus did. Not that I may be set as a judge over others, but that I may be used to bring life to those who do not have it. Let me show love to those who have not experienced it freely, and joy to those whose hearts are sullen. Through Jesus the Son. Amen.*

Week 3: Friday

John 5:31–40   Witnesses to Jesus' Authority

In the continued discourse on his authority, Jesus refers to a principle in the Law that calls for more than one witness in a civil case (Num. 35:30; Deut. 17:6, 19:15). If he were the only one testifying to his authority, he says, his word would be untrue. But he is not the only one. "There is another who bears witness" (v. 32). Some interpreters have taken this to mean John the Baptist, of whom Jesus speaks in the next verse. But the sense of the passage requires it to be God, for the reference to John is parenthetical to a longer reference to God. Jesus appears to think of John after mentioning God.

"You sent to John," he says, "and he has borne witness to the truth" (v. 33). Compare John 3:25–30, in which the Baptist said, "I am not the Christ, but I have been sent before him." Not that the word of a mere human being is adequate, says Jesus; he cites John's witness only because "the Jews" seemed to delight in him and because, if they could believe through him, they would be saved.

It is really the Father's testimony that counts most, and the Father has witnessed to Jesus' authority in three ways:

(1) By letting Jesus do the works he has done in their midst. The purpose of the signs has been to lead people to belief.

(2) By bearing personal witness to Jesus' sonship. The reference is possibly to John 1:32–33, in which the Spirit of God descended like a dove on the Son.

(3) By the witness of the scriptures, which foretold the coming of the Son and the things he would do.

"The Jews," however, are insensitive. They have seen the signs and wonders in their midst but have not believed. They cannot hear the voice of God and so do not accept God's confirmation of the Son. And, though they search the scriptures constantly, hoping to find eternal life, they miss the clues and do not come to the Son, who can give them life.

Lord, teach me to listen faithfully for your voice, that I may learn to trust it above my own opinions or the opinions of those around me. Let your witness be the measure by which I evaluate all other voices. For you have the words of eternal life. Amen.

Week 3: Saturday

John 5:41–47   The Glory of God

The Jews in Jesus' day accorded exceptional honor to famous rabbis, and many rabbis lived like princes among their country-men. They were given large banquets and were attended by the wealthiest citizens of whatever town they visited. Their words were repeated in the best society, and they were respected as the wisest men in the world.

The rabbis themselves contributed to this aura by the way they continually quoted one another's words and praised one another's sagacity. They had, as it has been called, a "mutual admiration society."

Jesus, as John indicates, did not take part in this self-serving exchange of praise. His glory was not the cheap demi-glow of human commendation, but the glory and honor of God him-self. Yet, because he did not play the little game the rabbis played, they did not speak well of him, and "the Jews" did not accept him.

"I know," said Jesus, "that you do not have God's love in you, for I have come in his name and you have refused to receive me. But if some rabbi comes among you in his own name, puffed up with human conceit, you fall over yourselves to receive him. You are full of pride, and love to exchange praise for one another instead of seeking the glory of God" (vv. 42–44, P).

What shame verse 44 strikes into our hearts if we but ponder it! For which of us is not guilty of having had more regard to what other persons think of us than what God thinks? Even in Christian congregations, we are often influenced more by what the minister or other well-placed persons think than by what God desires. We should commit this verse to memory and meditate on it often during the coming week.

The final verses of the passage contain added irony if the "feast of the Jews" in verse 1 was indeed the Feast of Pentecost, honoring Moses and the Law. "Don't think I am the one accusing you to God for your error," says Jesus. "It is your beloved Moses who accuses you, for he wrote of me and you do not believe him" (vv. 45–46, P).

Lord, I am certainly guilty of caring what others persons think of me. I know I have done things to receive their honor and good opinion when I should have done them for you and the kingdom alone. Forgive me, and restore a right spirit within me. Through Jesus, who knows what is in the hearts of people. Amen.

WEEK 4

Week 4: Sunday

John 6:1–14   Communion by the Sea

This is the only miracle of Jesus recorded by all four Gospels (Matt. 14:13–21; Mark 6:32–44; Luke 9:10–17), and John's account is probably the best loved, for it alone provides the detail about the small boy who surrendered his lunch to feed the multitude. The boy's example has been hailed again and again in sermon and story.

Actually, there are numerous significant details in the story, including the information that Passover was at hand. Passover was the most important Jewish feast, as it celebrated the escape of the Jews from bondage in Egypt and the subsequent founding of their nation. Even Christian Jews would have continued to attend special synagogue services and eat the Passover meal. Perhaps John's note about Passover in verse 4 was intended for these particular Jews, as a way of saying to them that, though they were no longer permitted to attend Passover services in the synagogues, Jesus had given Christians another meal, the Eucharist or communion, as a celebration of enormous significance.

Reminders of the Eucharist abound in the story. First, Jesus gave thanks over the bread. The Greek word for giving thanks, *eucharisteō*, is the very word from which the Eucharist derives its name. Second, Jesus himself distributes the bread, just as he will at the Last Supper. (In the Synoptic accounts, it is the disciples who do the distributing.) Third, the Greek word for fragments, *klasma*, is the same word used in the *Didache*, our earliest manual of church practice, for the eucharistic bread remaining after the meal. And, fourth, Jesus told the disciples to gather up the fragments "that nothing may be lost," foreshadowing a practice of conserving the leftover bread.

The multiplication of fish as well as bread is interesting. In Numbers 11, the Israelites are represented as complaining in the wilderness that they had only manna to eat. "O that we had meat to eat!" they cried (v. 4). Moses was despondent. "Where am I to get meat to give to all this people?" he asked. "For they weep before me and say, 'Give us meat, that we may eat.' . . . Shall all the fish of the sea be gathered together for them, to suffice them?" (11:13, 22) Is it possible that Jesus' giving the people both bread *and* fish was John's way of saying to Jewish Christians, "Here is one greater than Moses"?

The fact that the boy's lunch consisted of barley loaves and fish indicates a background of poverty. This may have symbolized the economic standing of the early Christians, many of whom were slaves and mendicants. Nevertheless, they were rich in Christ. He fed them until they had "eaten their fill"—and still there was an abundance left over. Twelve basketsful of fragments were collected, recalling the twelve tribes of Israel and the twelve disciples.

The reaction of the crowd is important. Following the miraculous sign, the people all acknowledged that Jesus must be "the prophet who [was] to come into the world." In popular belief, a prophet like Moses or Elijah would appear before the end, heralding a new age. And the appearance would occur at Passover. Unfortunately, as we shall see in the next reading, the people misunderstood the sign of the loaves and fishes. Jesus came as a spiritual leader, and they tried to make him a temporal king.

O Lord, I am thankful for John's inclusion of the small boy in this wonderful story. It reminds me of the way you can use my poor gifts if I will only yield them to you. Let me be as generous as the boy, I pray, that I may see miracles around me every day. In Jesus' name. Amen.

Week 4: Monday

John 6:15   The Temptation in the Wilderness

The Gospel of John does not contain a full-blown narrative of the temptation of Christ such as the one we find in Luke 4:1–13. Luke says that Jesus was led by the Spirit to the wilderness and tempted three times. First, he was challenged to turn stones into bread and satisfy his hunger. Second, he was taken to a high mountain and shown the kingdoms of the world. "If you will worship me," said the devil, "it will all be yours" (Luke 4:7). Third, the devil whisked Jesus to the pinnacle of the temple and bade him to test God's protection by throwing himself down.

The portrait of Jesus in the Gospel of John is of a confident, self-assured Christ almost above temptation. He is human enough to weep (11:35) and thirst (19:28). But he is also the eternal Word, and shows no signs of an inner struggle with the Tempter.

Yet this single verse (6:15) is a hint that John knew the tradition of the wilderness temptations, for it barely masks a temptation similar to the second temptation in Luke's account, to become a king without going through the horror of the cross. Curiously, too, it follows the story of the multiplication of loaves and fishes as the second temptation in Luke followed one associated with turning stones into bread.

The eloquence of John's statement lies in its terseness and simplicity. Jesus saw the mounting enthusiasm of the people for the miracle he had performed, and, not wishing to be a political king, withdrew to the mountain by himself. Some ancient manuscripts used the word *pheugei*—he actually *fled* to the mountains.

To understand the full irony of the verse, we must turn ahead to Jesus' trial before Pilate, in which he was accused of making himself King of the Jews (18:33–37). To Pilate's question "Are you the King of the Jews?" Jesus eventually responded, "My kingdom is not of this world." And later, when Jesus was crucified, Pilate defied "the Jews" by placing a sign on the cross that read "Jesus of Nazareth, the King of the Jews" (19:19).

The true qualities of royalty in any person are unrelated to the approval of the crowds. They are inner qualities, qualities in the bone and marrow. Jesus showed his character by refusing to be swept into a position of earthly power by people who did not understand his real mission among them. His retreat to the mountains, where he could be alone with the Father, ought to be an example for us whenever we are about to submit to a popular temptation. The real values of life are not found in the acclaim of the crowd but in the quiet of the lonely heart.

O God, in whose deep silences all truths become clear, teach me to depend less on my own wisdom and more upon yours. For you have ordained that poverty may be riches, weakness strength, and loneliness the ground of true companionship. Through Jesus Christ our Lord. Amen.

Week 4: Tuesday

John 6:16–21   Crossing the Sea

If you are familiar with parallel passages in Matthew 14:22–27 and Mark 6:45–51, you are probably disappointed in John's account of the storm at sea and Jesus' walking on the water. In the Synoptic versions, the disciples thought they were seeing a ghost on the water and cried out in terror. In Matthew, there is the added story of Peter's disastrous attempt to walk on the water to Jesus. And, in both Matthew and Mark, the winds suddenly died down when Jesus stepped into the boat.

Much of the drama seems to be missing in John's story. Jesus came walking on the sea. The disciples were frightened. Jesus said, "It is I; don't be afraid." They gladly received him into the boat, and—a curious detail—immediately "the boat was at the land to which they were going." It almost seems that John had no interest in the story and has condensed it in order to be quickly done with it.

Reflection, however, may convince us otherwise.

First, let's recall the total setting of the passage, within the feeding miracle (6:1–15), and the important discourse on the bread of life (6:25–59). All of this occurred, we are told in verse 4, at Passover time. The feeding story therefore had an obvious relationship to Jewish memories, always rehearsed at Passover, of God's having sustained his people with manna in the wilderness. Another significant Passover memory was of the crossing of the Red Sea, when God saved the Israelites from the pursuing Egyptian army. One of the synagogue readings for Passover was Isaiah 51:6–16. It included these verses:

> Was it not thou that didst dry up the sea,
>   the waters of the great deep;
> that didst make the depths of the sea a way
>   for the redeemed to pass over? (10)
>
> . . . .
>
> For I am the Lord your God,
>   who stirs up the sea so that its waves roar—
> the Lord of hosts is his name (15).

John's brief account of the stormy crossing, in other words, evoked powerful associations with the crossing of the Red Sea. For the New Israel, the church, it symbolized a moment of passage as important as the original crossing. Orthodox Jews might continue to celebrate the old crossing in their synagogues; Christians could celebrate the more recent crossing, and rejoice to know that the messiah was in the ship with them.

This brings us to another important detail in John's account—the *egō eimi* saying in verse 20. These Greek words, which occur also in the Synoptic versions, are usually translated "It is I." Literally, however, they mean simply "I am." We have commented earlier that they are reminiscent of God's self-identification to Moses in Exodus 3:14 as "I AM WHO I AM." "Say this to the people of Israel," God told Moses, "I AM has sent me to you." Of all the Gospels, John certainly lays most emphasis on the phrase *egō eimi*. His Jesus repeatedly employs the formula in introducing some facet of his messiahship—"I am the bread of life," "I am the resurrection and the life," "I am the door of the sheep," etc. It is impossible to read this passage about the storm at sea and not recognize in Jesus' "I AM" a declaration of power and transcendence, and an identification with the Father who has given him authority to perform signs and wonders.

Of course the disciples were "glad to take him into the boat"! They must have felt like the Jews described by Isaiah 51:11, in the Passover reading:

> And the ransomed of the Lord shall return,
>   and come to Zion with singing;

everlasting joy shall be upon their heads;
they shall obtain joy and gladness,
and sorrow and sighing shall flee away.

And what about the curious ending of the passage—
"immediately the boat was at the land to which they were going"? Is
that a mere fairytale touch—zip! and they were at their destination?
Or does it have a more esoteric meaning? Say, that they needed
wait no longer for the fulfillment of God's promises to Israel, for the
Savior had already come and was with them!

*O Lord, there are such spiritual depths in this small passage that I feel
like the disciples floundering in the waves. Let Christ come to me amid
the threatening waters and join me in my frail vessel, that I may not be
afraid, but may rejoice as the early Christians did, with singing and
everlasting joy. Amen.*

Week 4: Wednesday

John 6:22–40   A Sermon about Bread

It is impossible to believe that all five thousand people who were
fed from the barley loaves and fishes followed Jesus in boats across
the sea. They would have constituted a veritable armada! Probably
John meant to indicate that a group of them—possibly a few
dozen—took passage in some fishing boats and came looking for
Jesus on the other side of the lake.

When they found him, their first question was about how he
managed the crossing. They had seen the disciples leave in the only
boat the disciples had, and they knew Jesus did not sail with them.

Jesus' answer betrays the impatience he felt for their failure to
perceive the spiritual nature of his having fed them. "You seek
me," he said, "not because you saw signs, but because you ate your
fill of the loaves" (v. 26). That is, the miraculous healings (v. 2)
and the multiplication of loaves and fishes were not signs to them
because the events did not point beyond themselves to the mysteries
of the kingdom. The people merely saw in Jesus a perpetual meal
ticket—a king who could feed them even when food was scarce.

We should understand this, for we often behave the same way.

We too are more interested in having a government able to feed us—one that provides a favorable economic climate and a guaranteed income—than we are in the designs of God for our lives. Our stomachs carry a stronger vote than our souls.

"Don't spend your life's energies on the kind of food that perishes," said Jesus, "but seek the food that means eternal life for you" (v. 27, P). The Son of man will *give* us this imperishable food, he said.

Trying to understand, the people asked what they had to do to get the eternal bread. They were still trying to behave like their fathers, who had had to obey the laws of God for the manna in the wilderness. But Jesus told them what God's real work for them was—to believe in the Son who had come to them.

Like the simple folk they were, the people cited the only similar instance they knew—Moses' feeding of their fathers on manna in the wilderness. It was their recollection of this that had spurred them, the day before, to hail Jesus as a prophet and try to make him a king.

No, said Jesus, Moses did not give them the bread; God did. And it was God who was now trying to give them the true bread from heaven, not some mere sign such as the manna or the multiplication of loaves and fishes. "For the bread of God is that which comes down from heaven, and gives life to the world" (v. 33).

Apparently the people understood at last. "Lord, give us this bread always," they asked (v. 34).

In response to their humble supplication, Jesus spoke the words in verses 35–40.

"I am the bread of life," he said. "Whoever comes to me will neither hunger nor thirst. And I will keep that person and raise him up at the last day. For it is my Father's will that whoever sees the Son and believes in him have eternal life, and be raised up at the last day" (v. 35–40, P).

Lord, give me this bread, that I may neither hunger nor thirst. Help me to see beyond mere physical tokens to the food that is eternal. Let my praise be always for the gifts of the Spirit, more than gifts of the flesh. For they shall not perish or fail me. Amen.

Week 4: Thursday

John 6:41–59   The Mystery of the Bread

As the last verse indicates, this exchange between Jesus and "the Jews" occurred in the synagogue at Capernaum, not among the simple folk by the sea. Word had reached some of the elders of the synagogue that Jesus had said to the people, "I am the bread which came down from heaven."

"Why," they whispered among themselves as Jesus began to teach, "we know this man's background. He is the son of Joseph of Nazareth. How can he say that he came down from heaven?" (v. 42, P).

Jesus scolded them for murmuring. They couldn't understand, he knew, because God had not given them understanding; only those whom the Father drew could come to him. Like their fathers, who had eaten manna in the wilderness, they would die. But all of those who came to the Son believing would have eternal life.

The comparison of bread and manna was similar to the one in John 4, in Jesus' discussion with the woman at the well. There Jesus had said, "Every one who drinks of this water will thirst again, but whoever drinks of the water that I shall give him will never thirst" (4:13–14). Here, in this passage, Jesus said, "Your fathers ate the manna in the wilderness, and they died. This is the bread which comes down from heaven, that a man may eat of it and not die" (vv. 49–50).

Unlike the common people by the sea, who said, "Lord, give us this bread always" (v. 34), "the Jews" in the synagogue stumbled at the idea of Jesus' being bread and giving his flesh to eat. "How can this be?" they wanted to know. But they were unable to understand the mystery.

Let us remember again that John composed his Gospel especially for Jewish Christians being exiled from the synagogues. We can imagine the effect this passage had on them. It portrays the leaders of the synagogues as being dull and unperceptive, unable to grasp in faith the teachings accepted by the simple people at the seashore.

"You see," the passage said in effect to these Jewish Christians, "those in the synagogues do not understand the mysteries of our beliefs because God has not given them the gift of understanding. Our Eucharist is folly to them, for they do not see how a man born of human flesh can have come down from heaven. But we understand, and know that we have eternal life by eating the flesh and drinking the blood of Christ."

What a wonderful gift it is, Lord, to see you in the communion—to know, in some mysterious way, that when I eat the bread and drink the cup I am feeding upon you. Nourish me today that I may dwell with you forever. And let my life become food for others, for your name's sake. Amen.

Week 4: Friday

John 6:60–71   Some Disciples Go Away

The "hard saying" of verse 60 is the word of Jesus in verses 51–58 about eating his flesh and drinking his blood. The mystery of the sacramental body was anathema to Jews. Paul said the Cross was "a stumbling-block" for them (1 Cor. 1:23). They simply could not tolerate the idea of another human being's becoming a sacrificial lamb for them.

Even some of Jesus' disciples "murmured" about the saying (v. 61), as "the Jews" had in the earlier passage (v. 43). Jesus' question to them, "Do you take offense at this?" or, "Are you scandalized at this?," employs the verb from the same root as the noun Paul used in 1 Corinthians 1:23. They reacted as "the Jews" in the Gospel generally did.

The reference in verse 62 to the ascension is equivalent to saying, "What if you were to see the one who will die and give his flesh as an eternal meal rising to be with the Father? Then would you realize the connection between this bread and spiritual reality?"

"It is the spirit that gives life," said Jesus; "mere flesh doesn't understand such paradoxes. My words *are* spirit and life. But some of you still don't believe" (vv. 63–64, P).

The disciples Jesus was addressing were obviously a larger group than the twelve. Luke 10:1 refers to "the seventy." Probably these were the ones referred to in this section of John. But, after this confrontation about spiritual matters, many "drew back" and no longer followed—all of them, apparently, except the twelve.

John, in keeping with his heavenly image of Jesus, carefully points out that Jesus knew all along which disciples did not believe and which one would eventually betray him (literally, "hand him over"). We were told in 2:25 that Jesus "knew what was in man." Perhaps this is why the question in verse 67—"Will you also go away?"—is worded in the Greek to imply a negative answer. Jesus knew the twelve would remain, and that Judas would be the one to turn him over to the enemies.

What a sad picture, Lord, of the humanity you came to save. There is weakness and treachery in the best of us—even those who have been with you as disciples. The bright note is your own presence in our midst, manifested in the bread and wine of communion. Forgive our shortcomings and feed us on your eternal self, that we may not fall away or betray you. Amen.

Week 4: Saturday

John 7:1–13 Going to Jerusalem

The Gospel of John is much more centered in Jerusalem than the other Gospels. In the Synoptics, most of Jesus' ministry occurred in Galilee. John, with more than two-thirds of his Gospel to go, shifts our attention at this point to the ministry in Jerusalem. Jesus will go briefly to Transjordan (10:40) and spend some time at Ephraim near the desert (11:54), but there will be no further mention of his going to Galilee. The stage is already being set for his great conflict with the authorities and for the crucifixion.

It seems odd that Jesus' brothers should bait him to go up to Jerusalem for the Feast of Tabernacles—they did not believe in him despite the signs he had done—and that he should at first refuse to go. Raymond Brown has seen an interesting parallel between their urging the trip and the devil's third temptation of Jesus in Matthew 4:1–11 and Luke 4:1–13. The three temptations in the Synoptics were: (1) to rule the kingdoms of the world; (2) to turn the stones to bread; and (3) to display his power by leaping from the pinnacle of the temple in Jerusalem. In John 6:15, Jesus fled lest the people try to make him a king (temptation #1). In John 6:31, the people asked him for miraculous bread (temptation #2).

And, in the passage we are considering, his brothers tried to persuade him to go to Jerusalem and demonstrate his power (temptation #3).

Jesus' answer to his brothers was that his time had not come. The Greek word for time, *kairos*, is charged with theological significance. It means "fullness of time"—ripeness—as contrasted with another Greek word, *chronos*, which means mere clock or calendar time. In the Gospel of John, *kairos* is used almost interchangeably with the word "hour"; compare, for example, Jesus' words to his mother at the wedding in Cana, "My hour has not yet come" (2:4). The "hour" and the "time" would come at the same moment—when everything was ready.

Later, after the brothers had gone to Jerusalem, Jesus apparently decided that the time had come and went secretly to the city. This agrees with Mark 9:30–31, which reports that Jesus didn't want anyone to know he was going to Jerusalem and that he used the time on the journey to explain to the disciples that he would be killed there.

"The Jews" were expecting him at the feast. Probably they were already at work attempting to turn the populace against him. John says there was "much muttering about him among the people" (the word for "muttering" is the same one used in 6:41 and 6:61 for "murmuring," with a negative denotation). Some people insisted that Jesus was a good man, but others said he was deceiving people. Apparently this was a standard charge made against him. Luke 23:2 refers to it as the formal accusation against him in the trial before Pilate ("We found this man perverting our nation"), and Matthew 27:63 has the Pharisees telling Pilate that Jesus is an "impostor" or "deceiver."

The phrase "for fear of the Jews" in verse 13 sets the tone for the confrontations to follow. These particular Jews—obviously the authorities in Jerusalem—are seen as being both treacherous and powerful. They are emissaries of the darkness, and are naturally opposed to the light of the world. Conflict is inevitable.

O Lord, even your own brothers in the flesh did not understand you. What a dark and ignorant place the world is! How blind we can be to one another and to the truth! I pray for a light in the darkness, for even a glimmer to follow in my own personal dealings. Let me not fail to understand those close to me, for in serving them I am able to serve you, and in loving them I show my love to you. Amen.

62]

WEEK 5

Week 5: Sunday

John 7:14–36   The Greatest Rabbi of All

The Feast of Tabernacles lasted seven days, except when it began on a sabbath; when it began on a sabbath, it ran through the following sabbath, for a total of eight days. Jesus probably began to teach in the temple on the third or fourth day of the feast.

The people were amazed at the depth and perception of his teaching, particularly in light of the fact that he had studied under no other rabbi. In those days, men became rabbis by following other rabbis and learning to speak as they did. There was a standard rabbinical lore, consisting primarily of the sayings of famous rabbis. But Jesus exhibited none of the traditional lore; there was a freshness and incisiveness about his teachings. Luke 2:46–47 indicates that already at the age of twelve he was astounding the learned men of the temple. John did not bother to cite this detail, if indeed he knew it; for him, Jesus was the divine Wisdom incarnate in human form, and no other explanation was needed for his exceptional teachings. "My teaching is not mine," said Jesus, "but his who sent me" (v. 16).

In the course of his discussion, Jesus raised the issue of the plot to kill him. No plot had been made public, but Jesus knew of its existence as, in the Fourth Gospel, he knew other things. His enemies were caught off guard and said he was crazy—literally, that he had a demon, which at that time was the way of expressing dementedness.

Jesus pinpointed the reason for their hostility—it was the healing of the crippled man on the sabbath (5:2–18). "I did one deed," he said, "and it shocked you all" (v. 21, P).

Then Jesus used a rabbinical argument to justify the healing. The rite of circumcising a male child was supposed to occur on the eighth day after birth. If birth occurred on a sabbath, circumcision was permitted on the following sabbath (the eighth day, counting the first sabbath as day one). Circumcision affected only part of the body, though it was supposed to be efficacious for the total personality. Jesus' argument proceeded from a lesser to a greater benefit: if circumcision was permitted, why wasn't the healing of the whole body, which obviously did even more for the person affected? "Don't be superficial in your judgments about these matters," said Jesus; "really use your senses" (v. 24, P).

The people were confused. Jesus seemed so wise, so right, that it was hard not to believe he was the messiah. Yet they knew his family and where he came from. His brothers were right there in the crowds. Wasn't the messiah supposed to come in secrecy, from unknown origins? Nathanael had perhaps echoed a similar belief when he asked, "Can anything good come out of Nazareth?" (1:46)

"All right," said Jesus, in effect, "so you know me and know where I come from. But I don't come on my own. I was sent. And you *don't* know the One who sent me" (vv. 28–29, P).

It was an effective point, and carried the argument back to the center of the matter all along—that Jesus knew God and his enemies did not. Many people believed in him. "Could another messiah do more signs than this one?" they asked (v. 31, P). But the authorities intensified their efforts to arrest Jesus. Only the fact that his hour had not come deterred them; God would not give them the power they needed until the time was right.

Always in command, Jesus spoke words "the Jews" could not understand. "I shall be with you a little longer, and then I go to him who sent me; you will seek me and you will not find me; where I am you cannot come" (vv. 33–34). Later, he would speak the same words to the disciples in the upper room (13:33, 16:16). "The Jews" were confused. Was Jesus planning to escape from their territory and take up teaching in a Jewish colony elsewhere? Their minds were not spiritual enough to perceive that the one who had come from God was about to return to God.

> O God, I know how the authorities felt. I too have trouble with the fact that Jesus came from Nazareth and had a family like my own. But that is because my spirit, like theirs, is too earthbound and prosaic. When I am in prayer, and am no longer hindered by human rationality, I know he is the Christ, and that I am part of his kingdom. Grant that the mood of my praying may more and more dominate the rest of my life, that I may live for the kingdom every hour, and with every ounce of my being. For his name's sake. Amen.

Week 5: Monday

John 7:37–52   The Baptism of the Spirit

To understand the impact of Jesus' words on the final day of the feast, it is important to know a little about the feast itself. The Feast of Tabernacles, together with Passover and Pentecost, was one of three major Jewish festivals. Occurring in the autumn, it was associated with the harvest, but it also commemorated the years of wilderness wanderings, when the Israelites lived in tents or tabernacles. The people celebrated it with special religious services and by erecting small huts or booths reminiscent of the wilderness dwellings.

One of the central images of the feast was *water*. Finding water to drink had been a primary concern of the Israelites in the wilderness, and water for crops was always a concern after they reached the promised land. Therefore many of the scripture readings for synagogue services during the feast contained references to fountains, springs, and rivers. One reading, for example, Zechariah 9–14, describes the coming of the messianic king and God's giving men "showers of rain,/ to every one the vegetation in the field" (10:1). "On that day," said the prophet, "living waters shall flow out from Jerusalem, half of them to the eastern sea and half of them to the western sea; it shall continue in summer as in winter. And the Lord will become king over all the earth" (14:8–9).

In keeping with the emphasis on water, a special ceremony was observed during each morning of the feast. A procession descended from the temple to the fountain of Gihon, where a priest filled a golden pitcher with water as the choir sang Isaiah 12:3—"With joy you will draw water from the wells of salvation." Then the procession climbed the hill to the temple, singing the Hallel psalms (113-118), and marched around the altar in front as they sang:

> Save us, we beseech thee, O Lord!
> O Lord, we beseech thee, give us
> success! (Ps. 118:25)

Finally the priest mounted the ramp to the altar and poured the water into a silver funnel that allowed it to return to the ground. On the last day of the feast, the circling of the altar occurred not once but seven times.

It was probably at this moment on the final day of the feast ("the great day," as John calls it in verse 37) that Jesus stood up and cried out (the same verb is used for John the Baptist's crying out in the wilderness): "If anyone thirst, let him come to me and drink. He who believes in me, as the scripture has said, 'Out of his heart shall flow rivers of living water'" (vv. 37–38).

We can imagine the dramatic impact of such an announcement, especially at a time when the people were so divided in their opinions about Jesus and were talking about him constantly.

Curiously, there is no particular verse of scripture that says, "Out of his heart shall flow rivers of living water." Numerous theories have been proposed to explain the quotation. One of the Hallel psalms, 114, sung during the procession to the temple, says:

> Tremble, O earth, at the presence of the Lord,
> at the presence of the God of Jacob,
> who turns the rock into a pool of water,
> the flint into a spring of water (vv. 7–8).

The psalm's reference is to Moses' striking the rock and bringing forth water (Exod. 17:6, Num. 20:11). It is possible, too, that Jesus was referring to Zechariah 14:8, which we have already cited, "On that day, living waters shall flow out of Jerusalem."

Regardless of whatever scripture Jesus was citing, he probably adapted it in such a way as to refer to a phenomenon noted only in the Fourth Gospel, the issue of blood *and water* from the right side of the crucified (19:34). This would give meaning to "out of his heart" in the saying under question.

John, however, was untroubled by the source problem. He concentrated instead on the symbolism of Jesus' words. Jesus was really speaking, he said, about the pouring out of his Spirit on believers, which would occur after Jesus' death. Considering the fact that the outpouring of the Spirit occurred at Pentecost, when Jews from all over the Diaspora were gathered in Jerusalem, and thence reached many nations, John may indeed have been thinking of Zechariah 14:8 when he wrote Jesus' saying—on that day, living waters would flow out of Jerusalem to the east and the west!

When the temple police returned to the chief priests and Pharisees without Jesus, their leaders demanded to know why they had not arrested him. The police were unanimous in their reply: "No man ever spoke like this man!" (v. 46). The Pharisees were irate. Had the police found any inclination among them, the rulers of the people, to believe in Jesus? No, it was only the crowds who believed—the common people—and they were bewitched.

But one member of the Sanhedrin spoke courageously. It was Nicodemus, the ruler who had come to Jesus by night. Jesus had spoken to him about baptism "of water and the Spirit" (3:5). Did Nicodemus recognize a connection between that nocturnal conversation and Jesus' announcement at the feast about "rivers of living water" (v. 38)? Nicodemus' point was a telling one: their very Law provided for hearing a man before judging him (cf. Exod. 23:1 and Deut. 1:16–17). But the others were beyond reason. As tools of the darkness, they were trying to put out the light.

Lord, what a glorious scene this must have been, when you stood up at the feast and announced the "rivers of living water"! How prone I am to choke with thirst, when you are ready to provide your Spirit in measureless abundance. Help me this day to live with the image of the rivers, and to come to you repeatedly for my baptism of joy. Amen.

Week 5: Tuesday

John 7:53—8:11   The Woman Taken in Adultery

Most modern translations of the Fourth Gospel confine this passage to italics or small print to indicate its dubious place in the canonized text. No early manuscripts of reliability included it as a part of the Gospel. We are not certain precisely when it was inserted into the text, and some ancient manuscripts even place it in Luke, following 21:38, rather than in John. But through the centuries it has become a beloved part of the Gospel, told again and again to illustrate the tender forgiveness of Christ, and we shall do well to ponder it today regardless of its origin.

Verses 7:53 and 8:1 picture the disciples as going to various places of lodging about the city of Jerusalem, while Jesus went to his own place, somewhere on the Mount of Olives. Luke 21:37 says that "at night [Jesus] went out and lodged on the mount called Olivet," and this probably accounts for the passage's having been allocated in some manuscripts to this spot in Luke.

Early in the morning Jesus crossed the valley and climbed to the temple again, where he sat to teach. The day has always begun quite early for the people of Jerusalem, especially in the warmer months. They then become inactive at midday, when the temperature has risen, and resume a busier pace in the late afternoon.

The scribes and Pharisees brought a woman caught in the act of intercourse with a man who was not her husband. She was either an engaged woman or a woman already married, for the Law said nothing about adultery between a man and an unmarried woman who was not engaged. Leviticus 20:10 specified that both the man and the woman should be put to death, but in this case either the man was being held separately or he had escaped.

It is not clear whether the men who brought the woman to Jesus really intended to abide by whatever he decided about her. What *is* clear is that they expected to trap Jesus by whatever he said. If he said to release her, he would be countering a commandment of Moses; if he said she should be stoned, he would be in trouble with the Romans, who appear to have rescinded the Sanhedrin's power of capital punishment before this time. It was a dilemma similar to that of Mark 12:13–17, where Jesus was asked if it was lawful to pay taxes to Caesar.

68]

Jesus stooped down and wrote on the ground with his finger. What did he write? The question has puzzled interpreters through the ages. Perhaps he wrote the word "witnesses," and was thinking of Deuteronomy 17:7, which says, "The hand of the witnesses shall be first against him to put him to death, and afterward the hand of all the people. So you shall purge the evil from the midst of you." It was a text about a situation like this.

At any rate, Jesus stood and gave his judgment: "Let him who is without sin among you be the first to throw a stone at her" (v. 7). And once more he knelt to write on the ground.

One by one, beginning with the eldest, the accusers left. It is an interesting detail that the eldest went first. They, more than the younger persons, would understand the complexity of sin and evil in the world. As Georges Bernanos once wrote, "We inhale it in the very air we breathe."

Jesus looked up. "Where are they?" he asked. "Has no one condemned you?" "No one, Lord," she said. "Nor do I," said Jesus. "Go, and do not sin again" (vv. 10–11, P).

Some scholars believe this passage may have existed in the Fourth Gospel at an early stage and then been expunged for fear it would produce an air of easiness toward sin. Certainly it seems less astringent about morality than the letters of Paul and other early Christian writings. But Jesus did command the woman not to commit sin again, and the judgment he executed cut the accusers as well as the woman, suggesting that true morality is a matter the Law cannot finally regulate or guarantee.

There is one very good reason that we have not mentioned for the story's inclusion in the Fourth Gospel. That is its relationship to the Wisdom theme in John. The dilemma posed to Jesus was not unlike the one set before Solomon in 1 Kings 3:16–28, when two women claimed the same child. When Solomon solved the problem, the people stood in awe of him, "because they perceived that the wisdom of God was in him, to render justice." Many people have felt the same way about Jesus because of the sensitive way he handled the problem thrust upon him.

Teach me, O Christ, to number my own sins before counting the sins of others. Then let me wait upon your presence until I have received the judgment given to this woman. And I shall praise you for your great victory, which is from everlasting to everlasting. Amen.

Week 5: Wednesday

John 8:12–30   The Light on High

We are still dealing, in this section, with the Feast of Tabernacles, and again the ceremonies of the feast help us to understand
the text. Traditionally, *light* was important in the ceremonies in
much the same way that *water* was. The Israelites in the wilderness
had been guided by a pillar of fire by night. And Zechariah, who
provided a scriptural background for the water symbolism, likewise
said this about light in the coming Day of the Lord: "There shall be
continuous day (it is known to the Lord), not day and not night, for
at evening time there shall be light" (14:7).

As there was a ritual involving water during the time of
Tabernacles, there was one about light. It centered on the lighting
of enormous candles in the Court of the Women, an outer part of
the temple. There were four great golden candlesticks, each with
four golden bowls on top that were reached by ladder. Floating in
oil in these bowls were wicks made from the girdles of the priests.
When the wicks were lit, the light reflected by the burnished bowls
was said to illumine the entire city of Jerusalem.

It may well have been in the context of such a ceremony that
Jesus said, "I am the light of the world."

We can imagine the scene. The people were gathered in the
vicinity of the temple. Psalms were sung, and other scriptures were
recited. The priests chanted prayers. Then, at a climactic moment,
young men climbed the ladders and lit the special wicks. Out of the
hush of the crowd rose an exclamation of wonder as the highly
polished bowls caught the reflection of light and magnified it over
the night sky. Even people who had witnessed the lighting for years
were filled with awe.

And Jesus, standing among his disciples, spoke firmly and
assuringly, loud enough for others to hear: "I am the light of the
world; he who follows me will not walk in darkness, but will have
the light of life" (v. 12).

Once more we have an *egō eimi* saying—one of the great
messianic declarations of the Fourth Gospel. Like all the others, it
is only a partial statement of the nature and work of Jesus. But,
taken together, they imply the ultimate significance of his being.

70]

The Pharisees challenged the assertion. As before, they accused him of being his only witness. Even so, he said, it was enough, because he knew whence he had come and where he was going (that is, from and to the Father), and that gave special character to his witness. "You Pharisees judge things according to the flesh," said Jesus, "I don't. And I don't judge by myself. The One who sent me judges with me" (vv. 15–16, P).

(These verses about judging may account for the story of the adulterous woman's being placed next to them. Jesus' saying he judged no one according to the flesh would seem most appropriate to the story.)

Again Jesus spoke of going away (v. 21). This time, instead of supposing he was planning to slip away to the Diaspora, as in 7:35–36, "the Jews" wondered if he spoke of killing himself. They could not understand, because, as Jesus said, they were from below and he was from above; his actions and speech were indecipherable to them. Only if they believed on him would they not die in their sins.

"Who are you?" they asked him. I am who I have told you from the beginning, he said—the one sent by the Father. "When you have lifted me up"—the same verb is used as in 3:14–15, about lifting the serpent in the wilderness—"you will realize that I AM, and that everything I do, I do in the authority of the Father" (v. 28, P).

Yet again we have an *egō eimi*, only this time used without a predicate modifier. The New English Bible translation is "you will know that I am what I am," which I find preferable to the RSV and Jerusalem Bible's "you will know that I am he." But the real significance of the statement must be seen against God's word to Moses, "I AM WHO I AM," and, "Say this to the people of Israel, 'I AM has sent me to you'" (Exod. 3:14).

Here we see why the author of the Fourth Gospel equates Jesus' being lifted up with his being exalted or glorified. For, after his death, people would realize that he was who he had said he was from the beginning of his ministry, namely, the Son of the Father, the I AM himself. Then there would be no question about his authority or the testimony he gave. People would know he was "the light of the world."

Meanwhile, the Son's chief comfort was this: "He who sent me is with me; he has not left me alone" (v. 29).

I know, Father, what Jesus meant; I cannot bow before the cross without realizing his identification with you. There is a power and a mystery there that energizes my life with faith. Mediate your presence to me through that image, and help me always to follow him who was crucified and raised from the dead. In his great name. Amen.

Week 5: Thursday

John 8:31–59   A Greater than Abraham

There is some question about who is being addressed in this passage. Verse 31 says "the Jews who had believed on him." But it soon becomes obvious that these Jews are not faithful followers and, in fact, hold positions of hostility to Jesus. There are two possible explanations: (1) their belief evaporated ("they *had* believed on him") or (2) the addresses mysteriously shift, between verses 31 and 34, from Jews who believed to "the Jews" who had been Jesus' enemies all along. Whichever explanation we accept, the meaning of the passage is the same: only in Jesus, not in Abraham, is there freedom and life.

The statement in verse 33, "We are descendants of Abraham, and have never been in bondage to any one," is odd, for the Jews had been enslaved by the Egyptians and the Babylonians, and were at the very time of speaking under the rule of the Romans. Possibly the speakers were thinking of spiritual bondage, for it was true that Jewish worship had been maintained even under most exilic conditions.

Jesus' argument ran this way: (1) Anyone who sins is a slave to sin; (2) the Jews were trying to kill him, and were therefore sinners; (3) they were therefore also slaves.

Jesus accused "the Jews" of being children of the devil and not of Abraham. "We were not born of fornication," they exclaimed; "we have one Father, even God" (v. 41). No, said Jesus; if they had been children of God, they would have known him as the Son of God. As children of the devil, they were at home with lies, not the truth; that is why they did not recognize the truth of Jesus' words (vv. 43–45).

"The Jews" retorted by calling Jesus a Samaritan and saying he was possessed of a demon (v. 48). The reference to Samaritans may have been a slur implying that Jesus was not even a good Jew. To have a demon was to be deranged.

On the contrary, said Jesus, God would be the judge of who he was. And anyone who kept his word would never see death (vv. 49–51). Was he still speaking to "the Jews who had believed in him," trying to elicit their support?

"Now we know you are crazy!" said "the Jews." "Abraham died, as did all the prophets after him, and you speak of never tasting death. Who do you think you are? Are you greater than Abraham and the prophets?" (vv. 52–53, P)

"Ah," said Jesus, "Abraham. Abraham rejoiced to see my day. He saw it and was glad" (v. 56, P). The meaning of this is not clear. Jesus may have meant that Abraham foresaw the fulfillment of God's promises to him—that he would be the father of a great kingdom (Gen. 12:1–3)—in the kingdom of Jesus. Or, some interpreters believe, he may have spoken of Abraham after death, being able then to see all things clearly.

"The Jews" scoffed. "You are not yet fifty years old," they said. "How could you have seen Abraham?" (v. 57, P) Luke 3:23 says that Jesus was about thirty years old when he began his ministry. These are the only two scriptural references to Jesus' age. Only if the ministry was much longer than the chronologists have figured could Jesus have been near fifty when he died. The saying may have been mere exaggeration, without any attempt to fix upon his correct age.

Jesus' next remark was the climax of the discourse. "Truly, truly," he said, "before Abraham was, I AM" (v. 58). It is the *egō eimi* again, and again without a predicate modifier. There is extreme majesty in the announcement, as if to say, "Fifty years? A trifle. Before Abraham was born, I already existed."

At this, "the Jews" took up stones to throw at him. This probably does not imply a decision to execute him on the spot—the Jews did not have the power of imposing the death penalty. Instead, it suggests the irateness of their spirits. Jesus had provoked them beyond their limits, and, in exasperation, they picked up stones to throw at him.

But, as Jesus had slipped into Jerusalem secretly at the beginning of the feast, now he hid himself, possibly behind piles of stone or building materials being used to finish the temple, and slipped away. If any of the people he was addressing had been followers, there was no longer any question of where their sympathies lay. He left the temple alone.

Lord, all of this talk about Abraham is quite mystifying to me, for I was never a Jew. But I understand about slavery and freedom. Help me to believe in order that I may be free from the bondage of sin, and, being free, to praise your name at all times. Amen.

Week 5: Friday

John 9:1–12 The Light of the World and the Man Born Blind

This is one of the most delightful stories in the Gospel. Jesus, the light of the world, came into contact with a man who had never seen light and opened the man's eyes to the world around him. Later, when others asked the man what he thought about Jesus, he said, "He is a prophet" (v. 17); then, when Jesus questioned him, he said he believed that Jesus was the Son of man (vv. 35–38).

When the man was first encountered, the disciples asked a typical rabbinical question: Whose sin made the man blind, his or his parents'? Disregarding such a question as inconsequential— people are always more significant than philosophical disputes— Jesus replied that the important thing was to do God's work for the man while there was still time. "Night comes," he said, "when no man can work" (v. 4). Woven throughout Jesus' speech at this time were references to his crucifixion, when evil and darkness would seem to overcome the light.

So Jesus spat on the ground, made a bit of mud, and anointed the blind man's eyes with it. (In Mark 8:22–26 there is a similar account in which Jesus used spittle to heal a blind man.) Then he told the man to go and wash in the pool of Siloam. Why did the messiah who was able to heal the sick even at long distance (4:46–54) bother with this primitive method of healing?

Since Jesus' interview with Nicodemus in chapter three, there have been references in the Gospel to "water and the Spirit." Washing in the pool of Siloam almost certainly had baptismal significance in the eyes of first-century readers. In fact, the early church adopted this passage as part of the educational preparation of persons approaching baptism. Depictions of the story appear several times in catacomb art, always in connection with Christian baptism. The French scholar F.-M. Braun has discovered that during the years when the early church followed the practice of scrutinizing candidates three different times before admitting them to baptism, this chapter was read on the day of the final scrutiny.

The early church also made a connection between baptism and light. Candles were lit and handed to persons who had just been baptized, as a symbol of their enlightenment in Christ. And baptismal liturgies always contained numerous references to light and illumination.

The man who had been blind from birth, then, was made to see, and became an example to all of those seeking sight through faith in Jesus. Obediently, the man went to the pool and washed as he was told. And others were astounded at the change in the man. They argued among themselves (v. 9) about whether he was even the same man they had always known!

Lord, I wonder if my faith and baptism have made this much difference in how I live and how others perceive me. Do I behave as one who has seen a great light shining in the darkness? Open my eyes daily, I pray, to the magnificence of Christ, that I may not dwell with a shadowed spirit. In his bright name. Amen.

Week 5: Saturday

John 9:13–41 The Blindness of the Sighted

One of the great ironies of the Gospels is that those who are blind often see more than the sighted persons around them, while the sighted, who should see most, are spiritually blind. It is the same paradox as that encountered in the poor who are rich toward God and the rich who are impoverished in spirit.

In this passage we see the great contrast between the man who was blind from birth, yet came to see Jesus as the messiah, and the Pharisees, supposedly the most enlightened of Jews, who were unable to perceive the messiah who had done so many signs in their midst. They were angry with Jesus for other reasons, but here their anger focused on two points: (1) he had again violated the sabbath, both by mixing clay and by healing; and (2) he appeared to be doing the works of God, though they disputed his claim to be from God.

First, the Pharisees tried to disprove the miraculous nature of the healing by arraigning the man's parents and questioning them. There had been other cases of blind persons seeing again, but none where the persons had been blind from birth. The bent of the Pharisees' questioning was to discover whether the man had really been blind since birth. But the parents were adamant. This was their son, and he had been born without sight.

Then the Pharisees called in the man himself and tried to persuade him not to give credit for the healing to Jesus. "Give God the praise," they said; "we know that this man is a sinner" (v. 24). The implication was that no sinner could have done such a miraculous work. The man refused to be drawn into their dispute with Jesus. "I know what I know," he said, "—that I was blind and now I can see" (v. 25, P).

Like prosecutors grilling a witness, the Pharisees turned back to questions they had already raised. The man's wit was quick: "What's the matter with you," he asked in effect; "do you wish to become his disciples?" Incensed, the Pharisees accused the man of being one of Jesus' disciples. They themselves, they proudly declared, were disciples of Moses. They knew God had spoken to Moses, but they didn't even know where Jesus had come from. The man twitted them. They didn't know where Jesus was from, yet he had done the most wonderful work ever spoken of! If they had any sense at all, they would know Jesus had to be from God. Otherwise he could do nothing.

The Pharisees were irritated beyond their control. "You presume to instruct us," they said, "—you who were born in miserable sin!" (v. 34, P) This may have been a reference to the man's blindness from birth; they concluded that his sin produced the affliction. "And they cast him out."

Casting the man out, in light of verse 22, probably meant his ejection from the synagogue. Even in the time of Jesus, ruling Jews had the power to exclude people from synagogue worship, either for brief disciplinary periods or on a permanent basis. This would have been a permanent exclusion, and would have spoken eloquently to the Christian Jews of John's time who were facing expulsion from the synagogues unless they recanted and became non-Christians again. Indeed, John's intention in relating the entire narrative may well have been to encourage the followers of Jesus, who had been baptized (gone to the pool of Siloam) and received their sight (their Christian enlightenment) not to deny their faith under threat of excommunication from Jewish places of worship.

The final scene between the man and Jesus summarizes the situation. The man who had been blind from birth could now see. What he saw clearly was that Jesus was the Son of man, the long-awaited messiah. And the Pharisees, who made such a point of being able to see life clearly and discriminately, were really blind to the most important thing in the world, the lordship of Jesus.

It frightens me, O God, to be a leader of others—a parent, a teacher, a professional—and have a reputation for seeing. For it is in my contentment with this reputation that I am in most danger of not seeing—of being short-sighted, prejudiced, and wrong in my judgments. Teach me to rise each day and, recalling my darkness, humbly seek the light of Christ in my life. For he alone has seen you and knows the meaning of everything. Amen.

WEEK 6

Week 6: Sunday

John 10:1–21   The Beautiful Shepherd

This passage is related to the foregoing narrative in chapter nine by references to thieves, robbers, and hirelings who do not care for the sheep but steal and slaughter them (vv. 1, 8, 10, 12–13). Jesus was surely thinking of the Pharisees who did not care for the man born blind, but were willing to sacrifice the poor and afflicted for the sake of mere rules and regulations.

He probably had in mind also Ezekiel 34, which begins: "The word of the Lord came to me: 'Son of man, prophesy against the shepherds of Israel, prophesy, and say to them, even to the shepherds, Thus says the Lord God: Ho, shepherds of Israel who have been feeding yourselves! Should not shepherds feed the sheep?'" (vv. 1–2). Aileen Guilding, in her book *The Fourth Gospel and Jewish Worship*, says that this text regularly served as one of the prophetic readings for the Feast of Dedication mentioned in John 10:22. Therefore, just as ceremonials at the Feast of Tabernacles provided the background for Jesus' announcements in chapter seven ("If any one thirst, let him come to me and drink") and chapter eight ("I am the light of the world"), the reading for the Feast of Dedication prompted his discourse on shepherding.

The accusation in Ezekiel denounces the shepherds of Israel for not healing the sick, binding up the crippled, or seeking the lost. Because the shepherds have sought only their own welfare, it says, God will take away their shepherding function and assume it himself. "I myself will be the shepherd of my sheep, and I will make them lie down, says the Lord God. I will seek the lost, and I will bring back the strayed, and I will bind up the crippled, and I will strengthen the weak, and the fat and the strong I will watch over; I will feed them in justice" (34:15–16).

It was in the setting of these words that Jesus announced his role as shepherd of Israel. "I am the beautiful shepherd," he said, "the one who lays down his life for the sheep" (John 10:11, P). Most translations offer the wording "the *good* shepherd," but the word *kalos*, which they translate "good," also means "beautiful." We have a derivation of the word in the English "calligraphy," which means "beautiful writing." The sense of "beautiful" in the text is "perfect," "right," "exemplary." In other words, Jesus was the shepherd Ezekiel had promised, who would truly care for the sheep of Israel.

The reference to "the door of the sheep" or "sheep-gate" in verses 7 and 9 seems an intrusion into the shepherd metaphor. Possibly it was a separate utterance of Jesus edited into the sayings about shepherding because of its apparent affinity. Some interpreters have attempted to reconcile the images by suggesting that the shepherd lay down in the doorway at night to guard the sheep, thus becoming in effect the "door" to the sheep. This would certainly harmonize with the saying that the beautiful shepherd lays down his life for the flock.

There was a real intimacy, Jesus suggested, between him and the members of his flock. "I know my own and my own know me, as the Father knows me and I know the Father" (vv. 14–15). The sheep recognize the shepherd's voice and follow him when he calls them (v. 3). If the people were not following the Pharisees, it was because the Pharisees were thieves, robbers, and hirelings—not true shepherds.

Verse 16 has long taxed the imagination of commentators: "I have other sheep, that are not of this fold; I must bring them also, and they will heed my voice. So there shall be one flock, one shepherd." Given the audience of Jewish Christians to whom John was writing the Gospel, these words may well have meant that Jesus had followers in many places, not only among Jews in the synagogues, and that he would eventually bring them all together

into a single flock. Then there would be "one flock, one shepherd."
(The Greek is a clever play on words, for "flock" is *poimnē* and
"shepherd" is *poimēn*; hence one *poimnē*, one *poimēn*.)

The emphasis on the smitten shepherd is strong in the passage
because Jesus was approaching the time of his death. The Feast of
Dedication was in December; Jesus was crucified at Passover in the
spring. But references to resurrection and ascension were also
strong. "I lay down my life, that I may take it again. No one takes it
from me, but I lay it down of my own accord. I have power to lay it
down, and I have power to take it again; this charge I have received
from my Father" (vv. 17–18). John is the Gospel of *life*, not death.
The shepherd would be slain for the sheep; but even in death he
would prove triumphant.

> O *beautiful Shepherd, who laid down your life for me, I want to
> follow you wherever you lead. With you, even barren places become lush
> pastures, and the valley of the shadow of death becomes a field of
> resurrection!* Amen.

Week 6: Monday

John 10:22–42   The Consecrated One

The Feast of Dedication *(Hanukkah)* celebrated the victory of
Judas Maccabeus over the Syrians. In 167–164 B.C., the Syrians
erected an idol on the altar of the temple, constituting what the
Jews called "an abomination of desolation" (Dan. 9:27). When the
Maccabeans defeated the Syrians, a new altar was built and the
temple was rededicated. The memory of this important occasion
was relived annually in the Feast of Dedication.

Against this background, it is interesting that Jesus, confronting
"the Jews," referred to himself as the one "whom the Father
consecrated and sent into the world" (v. 36). The word for
"consecrated" is the same one used for consecrating an altar or a
temple. Jesus, at a time when Jewish minds turned to the
consecration of holy places, offered himself as the holy person
dedicated by God himself.

"How long will you keep us in suspense?" asked "the Jews." "If you are the Christ, tell us plainly" (v. 24). They did not want to know if he was the Christ; he had already told them as much, and, besides, they could see the works he did. They wanted him to make an official claim, so they could hail him before the authorities.

"You don't believe me," said Jesus, "because you are not part of my flock. My sheep know me, and follow me. I give them what you cannot have, eternal life, and will keep them forever. My Father joins me in protecting them, because he and I are one and the same" (vv. 27–30, P).

At this declaration of unity with the Father, "the Jews" picked up stones to hurl at him, just as they had when he said he existed before Abraham (8:59). For which of his "beautiful works" (again it is the word *kalos*) were they going to kill him? It was not for the works, they said, but for the blasphemy—making himself God.

Jesus stayed the barrage of stones by engaging "the Jews" in a rabbinical argument. He cited Psalm 82:6,

> I say, "You are gods,
>   sons of the Most High, all of you;
> nevertheless, you shall die like men,
>   and fall like any prince."

The setting of the speech, made by God, was in a paganlike council of gods, where the gods were guilty of aiding the strong and not the weak. God turned to the other deities present and denounced them for their injustice. They might be gods, he said, but they would die like human beings.

If God called even minor deities "gods," Jesus was arguing, why should "the Jews" think he was blaspheming—he whom the Father had set apart and sent into the world—when he said he was the Son of God? If his works were not the Father's works, then they should not believe him; but if the works were what the Father would do, then they should understand that he was who he said he was.

"The Jews" tried to arrest Jesus, we are told, but he escaped again as on previous occasions (7:30, 44), because his hour had not come. He went into Transjordan, to the area where John had baptized, and for a while enjoyed the acceptance of the simple people of the land.

Lord, I want to be a simple person. Remove all my pretension and unnecessary complexity. Let me meditate on you until all of my life is focused and plain. And then let others see you through me, shining through the aperture of my faith. For your kingdom's sake. Amen.

Week 6: Tuesday

John 11:1–44 The Resurrection and the Life

In the previous message (10:22–42) Jesus spoke about doing the works of the Father. In an earlier discourse, he had told "the Jews": "As the Father raises the dead and gives them life, so also the Son gives life to whom he will" (5:19–24). Here, in the present passage, we see the most dramatic picture of this life-giving mission in the entire Gospel and we reach the climax of all the *egō eimi* sayings, when Jesus declares, "I am the resurrection and the life" (v. 25).

This chapter is pivotal to the Gospel. The raising of Lazarus was the most important sign Jesus could give, for death is the final enemy of man. It was therefore natural, once the sign had been given, that it should intensify the opposition to his ministry and his antagonists should seek ways not only of arresting him but of putting him to death.

John wished, in this unusual story, to emphasize three things: Jesus' love for his friends, the absolute deadness of Lazarus, and the immediacy of life in Christ.

(1) *Jesus' love for his friends.* Mary, Martha, and Lazarus lived in the small hillside village of Bethany, scarcely two miles from Jerusalem. Luke mentioned that Jesus visited in Martha's house while Mary also was present (10:38–42). And John, anticipating his own narrative in the next chapter (12:1–3), identified Mary as the one who anointed Jesus' feet with precious ointment. All the references indicate that there was a close personal relationship between Jesus and these three persons in Bethany, and that it was probably natural for him to visit them when he was in the area of Jerusalem. Mark 11 suggests that during the final week of his life he taught in Jerusalem by day and returned to Bethany each evening. It was not extraordinary, therefore, that the two sisters sent to Jesus when their brother lay gravely ill. They knew Jesus had strange powers, and they believed he could heal their brother. Jesus was

touched by the message. John noted that he loved the three friends. The proof of his love was his willingness to go back to Bethany so soon after "the Jews" had tried to stone and arrest him. "Rabbi," said the disciples, "the Jews were but now seeking to stone you, and are you going there again?" (v. 8). Apparently the family was well known in Jerusalem, and the disciples knew there would be many people from the city coming to see them. But Jesus had recently said that "the beautiful shepherd lays down his life for the sheep" (10:11). There was no question about his going back!

An additional evidence of Jesus' love and humanity was his weeping at Lazarus' tomb (vv. 33–35). Commentators have long sought to explain why he wept though he knew he would raise Lazarus from the dead. Some have suggested that he wept at the human situation, so filled with grief; others, that he wept for the dead man's sake, that Lazarus should have to come back to this life after tasting the one beyond. But regardless of the reason, the fact that Jesus wept at the tomb of a friend is an eloquent touch in the portrait of the eternal Word who became fully human.

(2) *The absolute deadness of Lazarus.* In none of Jesus' other resuscitation miracles was such care taken to emphasize the full reality of death's presence. John wished there to be no doubt of Lazarus' deadness or of Jesus' power to raise the dead. Instead of responding immediately to the sisters' message about their brother's illness, Jesus purposely tarried until the brother was not only dead but "in the tomb for four days." He had been no more than thirty or thirty-five miles away, yet procrastinated until there was no doubt of Lazarus' demise. Other touches confirm the presence of death: the stone rolled across the mouth of the tomb, the wailing of the mourners, the bandages on the corpse, and Martha's warning that, if they rolled away the stone, there would be an odor, because Lazarus had been dead four days. This was no case of mere revival a few minutes after death; Lazarus was firmly in the grip of death.

(3) *The immediacy of life in Christ.* This was the major point of the entire story, as of the Gospel itself. Jesus did not respond immediately to the sisters' plea for help because he wished to provide the greatest sign of his power and purpose as the messiah. Not even the sisters understood his power. When he arrived, he saw them in turn, and each lamented that if he had only been there their brother would not have died (vv. 21, 32). To Martha, who was the first to greet him, he said, "Your brother will rise again" (v.

23). Martha replied with the common faith of those who believed in the resurrection at the time, "I know that he will rise again in the resurrection at the last day" (v. 24). But Jesus was going to show her something better than that. "I am the resurrection and the life," he declared; "he who believes in me, though he die, yet shall he live, and whoever lives and believes in me shall never die" (vv. 25–26). Going to the tomb, and pausing to give thanks for always being heard by God, he cried out into the hollowness of the burial vault, "Lazarus, come out!"

"The dead man came out," says the scripture, still emphasizing his deadness, "his hands and feet bound with bandages, and his face wrapped with a cloth."

"Unbind him," said Jesus, "and let him go" (vv. 43–44).

Nowhere in the Gospels is there a more stunning story—or one more central to the purposes of the Incarnation. Christ is clearly the resurrection and the life!

> *O Christ, my rational mind is shocked by this story; it is like nothing I experience in daily life. Yet its very outrageousness convinces me of its truth, and of the fact that I should experience it in daily life. Help me to know you so intimately through prayer and meditation that even my rationality shall come to understand and glorify you. For you are the Lord of both life and death. Amen.*

Week 6: Wednesday

John 11:45–57 A Misuse of Authority

In John's Gospel, people judged themselves according to their reaction to Jesus. Here is a primary example of this theological truth. The raising of Lazarus was Jesus' greatest sign of his union with the Father. Yet the members of the Sanhedrin, the council of Jewish elders, instead of accepting Jesus' messiahship, intensified their efforts to accomplish his death.

Like any group of "responsible citizens," the chief priests and Pharisees of the Sanhedrin cloaked their designs in civic respectability. They were worried about what the Romans would do if Jesus continued to perform miracles and recruit followers. The

Romans might become nervous, it was argued, and destroy the temple; or they might even lay waste the entire nation. We can almost hear the clacking of voices as the old men discussed their "duties" under the present state of emergency!

In the end, it was the words of the high priest that summed up the council's will: Jesus must die in order to avert a national disaster. Those words, "it is expedient for you that one man should die for the people, and that the whole nation should not perish" (v. 50), became an important preaching text to the early Christians. Caiaphas did not know how truly he spoke, or that what he had said would be given a spiritual interpretation by future generations.

The decision of the Sanhedrin to go all out in seeking Jesus' life was supposed to be a judgment on Jesus. As it turned out, it was a judgment on the council members themselves. How many times, in how many places, have people in authority committed a similar transgression of justice because some individual or group of individuals constituted a threat or an affront to their positions or self-interest? Even parents are prone to misuse authority in this way, as a means of bolstering the self and its ways.

As his opposition intensified, Jesus continued to be careful, waiting for the hour when he would give his life for his sheep. John says he went to a town called Ephraim, near the wilderness—a place so remote that scholars today argue over which small village it may have been. There he stayed with the disciples until the Feast of Passover. And, in Jerusalem, suspense was building among the people. The word was out that the Sanhedrin was set to arrest Jesus. Would he dare to come for the feast?

Lord, I know I have been guilty of abusing my authority as a parent, as a teacher, as a minister. I do it without thinking. There is a question, someone steps out of line, I haven't the time or energy to deal with the crisis, and I swing my weight. I have injured not only those with whom I was peremptory, but myself as well. Even worse, Lord, I have injured you. Forgive my self-centeredness and help me to be more constantly loving and considerate. For no position is worth the smallest act of inhumanity or the least betrayal of your trust. Amen.

Week 6: Thursday

John 12:1–8   A Prophetic Anointment

Accounts similar to this one are contained in Mark 14:3–9 and Luke 7:36–38. In Mark, the anointing occurs two days before Passover, in the house of Simon the leper, a resident of Bethany, and is performed not on Jesus' feet but on his head. In Luke, it occurs in Galilee, during the ministry there, at the home of Simon the Pharisee, and is done by a nameless sinful woman who first weeps on Jesus' feet, dries the tears with her hair, and then anoints his feet with perfume. Scholars have strained themselves to harmonize these accounts with the narrative in the Fourth Gospel, but with only modest success. John tells the story with his own set of details (the names of Mary, Martha, and Lazarus, and Judas' anger about the waste are found only in his version) and for his own theological purposes.

The suggestion has been offered, attempting to reconcile John with Mark's information about a dinner at Simon's house, that Simon was the father of Mary, Martha, and Lazarus. That is a plausible suggestion, and would account for Martha's serving at table. Martha's serving and Mary's act of worship also accord well with Luke's portrait of the two sisters (10:38–42), in which Martha "was distracted with much serving" while Mary "sat at the Lord's feet and listened to his teaching."

Here the action centers on Mary's sacrifice of a pound of nard on Jesus' feet. Nard, also known as "spikenard," was a kind of perfume extracted from the roots and spikes of the nard, a plant that still grows in northern India. It was, as the text indicates, extremely expensive, and was used sparingly in various perfumes, medicines, incenses, and burial lotions.

If a denarius was worth a day's wages, as we are informed by Matthew 20:2, then the flask of nard Mary used was worth nearly a year's wages. Judas, as keeper of the disciples' treasury, was understandably dismayed at the extravagance. He was not identified, in Mark's Gospel, as the one who objected; there the text says, "There were some who said to themselves indignantly, 'Why was the ointment thus wasted?'" (14:4). Either John represents a further development of the story in which Judas was purposely vilified or John had personal knowledge of Judas' objection which the other

Gospel traditions did not have. The former may have been true, for John has all along portrayed Judas as a devil (6:70) and will say in 13:2, 27, that he was cohabited by Satan. John alone among the Gospel writers gives the information that Judas was a thief and was accustomed to stealing from the group's money box (v. 6).

Jesus' comment in verse 7 that the anointment was for his burial indicates the prophetic nature of Mary's act. He would soon die for his beloved sheep. That it was a prophetic gesture would explain why Mary anointed his feet instead of his head, as in Mark. Perfume was normally put on the head or face to give a pleasant aroma to the person wearing it. A corpse, on the other hand, might be anointed on the feet as well as the head, for in the case of the dead the aroma was for other persons to smell, not the one who had died.

Some persons have been troubled by Jesus' apparent nonchalance about the poor in verse 8, "The poor you always have with you, but you do not always have me," and point out that this statement is much unlike Jesus' usual sentiments about the poor. Joachim Jeremias, however, has helpfully called attention to a distinction in rabbinic thought between two kinds of good works— those pertaining to mercy (including the burial of the dead) and those pertaining to justice (including alms for the poor). Actions related to mercy were always considered more important than those related to justice. Jesus was confirming an acceptable standard of piety, not a single action that happened to benefit him.

One important factor in Mary's behavior must not be overlooked, and that is the raising of Lazarus as narrated in chapter eleven. Mary could well part with the valuable perfume she was saving for her own burial because *she no longer felt the need of it.* Jesus had raised her brother from the dead. He had said, "I am the resurrection and the life." In a wonderful display of faith, she was "wasting" the precious ointment reserved for her funeral preparations, confident that Jesus had made it unnecessary. In what better way could she demonstrate her newfound understanding that he was the Lord of eternal life? The fact that Judas did not see the "logic" of her gesture meant that he was one of the sons of darkness. Like the Pharisees and high priests, he belonged to the evil one.

O God, I have always admired the spontaneity and generosity of Mary's act and wished that I could behave as she did. Now that I see her

[87

motivation—the transforming of life under the Prince of resurrection—
perhaps I can be like her. Let me see what she saw, I pray, that I may be
as she was. Through Jesus, who lives eternally. Amen.

Week 6: Friday

John 12:9–19   The Falseness of the Crowds

These verses are like little winds gusting before a storm. They
contain the mounting tension and frenzy of the final days before
Jesus' crucifixion.

First, we are shown the crowds that came to Bethany to see Jesus
and Lazarus. Lazarus had become a tourist attraction; no one had
ever before heard of a dead man raised to life, much less beheld
one. This provoked the authorities in Jerusalem to connive to put
Lazarus to death again. Merely being associated with Jesus was
becoming dangerous.

Then we see the crowds in Jerusalem—the thousands of pilgrims
who had arrived for Passover—going out to meet Jesus as he came
down the road from Bethany. They brought palm branches,
probably imported from the Jordan Valley for the Passover
ceremonies, and greeted him with words from Psalm 118:26–27—

> Blessed be he who enters in the
>   name of the Lord!
> We bless you from the house of the Lord.
> The Lord is God,
>   and he has given us light.
> Bind the festal procession
>   with branches,
>   up to the horns of the altar!

The last sentence may have been a liturgical direction not
originally part of the psalm. It would explain the appropriateness of
the palms. They were used to welcome pilgrims to the temple. In
the Palm Sunday context, however, Jesus was no mere pilgrim. He
was the Son of God, the spiritual King of Israel, and, in a sense
anticipated by the psalm, the light of the world.

The phrase "even the King of Israel" is not part of Psalm 118. It is probably a reference to Zephaniah 3:14–20, which includes the promise, "The King of Israel, the Lord, is in your midst," and speaks of a time when the lame will be cured and the outcasts gathered together.

In parallel passages in Matthew 21:8, Mark 11:8, and Luke 19:36, the crowds spread their cloaks and (in Matthew and Mark) the palm branches on the road before Jesus, giving an air of triumphalism to the entry. John does not mention the cloaks or the laying down of palm branches. In his Gospel, Jesus has been in Jerusalem many times, and John is less concerned with a triumphal entry than with the drama to come.

Verse 15 is a prophecy from Zechariah 9:9 that Israel's king would come riding on the foal of an ass. The comment in verse 16 that the disciples understood the significance of this only later, after Jesus had been glorified, is indicative of the early Christians' process of assimilating all that had happened: they recalled what had occurred and was said during Jesus' ministry and reflected on it in the light of scripture.

Reflecting on Jesus' entry into Jerusalem, John realized that many of those who cried "Hosanna!" were also in the crowd that shouted "Crucify him!" They went out to greet Jesus, not because they understood him to be the Son of God, but because they heard he was a miracle-worker. Crowds often follow a good show. The Pharisees despaired, however, when they saw the crowds. "Look," they said, "the whole world has gone after him" (v. 19). John saw the irony of this. Jesus' real hour of glory would be when he was lifted up on a cross and the crowds had fallen away—not now, when they were running to greet him.

O Christ, I am so easily blinded by the world's values that I fail to understand what is eternal and true. Teach me to see the world as you saw it, through the eyes of God, that I may not waste my time and energy pursuing the things that will neither last nor matter. For your name's sake. Amen.

Week 6: Saturday

John 12:20–36   The Arrival of Jesus' Hour

Throughout the Gospel, there have been references to Jesus' "hour" (2:4, 7:30, 8:20) and his "time" (7:6, 8). Now the hour has finally come. Jesus is ready to enter the fatal confrontation with the authorities in Jerusalem and to lay down his life for his sheep.

Perhaps the coming of the Greeks signaled the moment he had been waiting for. They came first to Philip, possibly because he would have spoken Greek, and asked to see Jesus. It must have been regarded by Philip as a momentous occasion, for he did not go directly to Jesus. Instead, he consulted his brother Andrew, and together they went to tell Jesus. The suggestion is that Jesus was in hiding, as he had been on other recent occasions (8:59; 10:40, 11:54), and the disciples felt some uncertainty about whether to take the strangers to him. We don't know if the Greeks ever did see Jesus. John was not interested in pursuing the story. What he cared about was the fact that Jesus saw their coming as an indication that his time had come to be lifted up.

Jesus' metaphor to the disciples about a grain of wheat falling into the ground and dying was an important lesson. He would be their great example, and they would later learn to give their lives as he gave his. "What good is saving your life," he asked in effect. "If you do that, you destroy it. It is only by living generously—by sowing your life profligately, as wheat is sown—that you enable the future to spring from your deeds!"

Jesus had come to this hour to die and be lifted up. It would have been pointless to flee, now that the hour was upon him. Instead, he prayed, "Father, glorify thy name." There was a sound like thunder. Those who were merely part of the crowd attracted by the raising of Lazarus assumed it was indeed thunder. But those who had faith said otherwise; they heard a voice say, "I have glorified it, and I glorify it again" (v. 28).

As Jesus had told Nicodemus that the Son of man must be lifted up like the serpent in the wilderness (3:14), now he repeated the necessity of his being lifted up in crucifixion (v. 32). The crowd, as usual, was uncomprehending. How could the Son of man be lifted up? Surely the real messiah would be above such a natural death.

Jesus' answer was simple: Walk in the light while you can, and become children of the light.

John had said in the prologue to the Gospel, "In him was life, and the life was the light of men. The light shines in the darkness, and the darkness has not overcome it" (1:4–5). In a little while, the light would seem to waver and go out.

Father, it takes a lot of living to understand what Jesus meant about dying. In selfishness, I try to preserve my life; but the minute I do that, I lose something. Teach me to live generously, loving the world as you have loved it. Then I shall not fear dying, or that I am leaving anything behind, for it will all be invested in you, who have never suffered any good thing to be lost. Amen.

WEEK 7

Week 7: Sunday

John 12:37–50   A Time for Summing Up

In the year of King Uzziah's death, Isaiah had an unforgettable experience of the mystery of God. He was in the temple and had a vision of God sitting on his throne. God's train—his retinue of angels—filled the entire temple. The angels were singing "Holy, holy, holy is the Lord of hosts," and when God spoke the very foundations of the doors trembled.

Afterwards, God sent Isaiah to speak to the Israelites. He was to say to them:

> Hear and hear, but do not understand;
> see and see, but do not perceive (Isa. 6:9).

God wanted Isaiah to make the people's ears heavy and cause them to shut their eyes,

> lest they see with their eyes,
> and hear with their ears,
> and understand with their hearts,
> and turn and be healed (6:10).

The people were already condemned by their sinfulness; God merely wished to increase their condemnation for not seeing and hearing.

John understood the Jews' failure to receive the Son of God in the framework of Isaiah's experience. He too, like Isaiah, had seen something almost beyond description—the incarnation of the eternal Word and a ministry filled with signs and wonders. Yet people had callously behaved as if Jesus were no more than a wandering magician. Their eyes beheld the glory of the Son of God, but they did not see him for who he was.

Some members of the Sanhedrin, John knew, believed Jesus was the Son of God. Nicodemus (3:1–14) was probably one of these. Joseph of Arimathea (Mark 15:43) was another. But they were afraid of being ejected from the synagogue if they confessed what they believed. They cared more for their reputations among men than for their reputation with God (v. 43). Worrying about what others think, John knew, could be spiritually fatal. "How can you believe," he wrote in 5:44, "who receive glory from one another and do not seek the glory that comes from the only God?"

Words like these must have scored a direct hit on people who were afraid of being expelled from their synagogues if they confessed to belief in Christ. Their fears would have put them in the class with the high-ranking Jews who never crossed over the line to become true disciples of Jesus.

Jesus' words in verses 44–50 are a kind of summary of what he has taught to this point of the Gospel. Many interpreters think they are out of place here, for Jesus has gone into hiding again (v. 36) and there is no one to hear them. But John saw them as an appropriate recapitulation before commencing the Passover narrative.

Those who believed in Jesus were really believing in the One who sent him. He was the light of the world, and those who followed him would not walk in darkness. He did not judge people, but people judged themselves by how they responded to him. And nothing he said was his own word, but was given to him by the Father.

The hardest part, for John, was to understand how people could see and hear what they had seen and heard, and still not believe.

Lord, I too am guilty of seeing and hearing and not believing. Your signs and testimonies in my life have been amazing, and have caused me to say again and again that I believe. Yet I live my life as if this were not so—as if I had seen and heard nothing. Forgive me, Lord, and let me stand once more in your presence. Renew an excited spirit within me. And this time help me not to forget so quickly. For your kingdom's sake. Amen.

Week 7: Monday

John 13:1–20   Sent by the Master

The tradition has been to read this passage principally as a narrative about humility: Jesus washed the disciples' feet, and we all should treat others in the same self-effacing manner. But interpreters in recent years have noted several difficulties in the passage. Three of these difficulties have to do with (1) the date of the Lord's Supper, (2) the significance of the foot-washing, and (3) the relationship of the washing to Judas the betrayer.

(1) *The date of the Lord's Supper.* The Synoptic Gospels clearly indicate that the meal eaten by Jesus and the disciples was a Passover meal. John says it was eaten "before the feast of the Passover" (v. 1). Later, John will allude to the day of crucifixion as the day of preparation for the Passover (19:14). Pilate handed Jesus over to the Jews for crucifixion at noon that day—the very hour when the priests were slaying the Passover lambs. Either there was a misunderstanding about the date—meaning that John or the Synoptic tradition was incorrect—or John purposely rearranged the date to give it a special theological significance. John the Baptist, upon seeing Jesus, had exclaimed to his disciples, "Behold, the Lamb of God, who takes away the sin of the world!" (1:29) By having the Last Supper *before* Passover and shifting the crucifixion to the day of preparation, the author of the Fourth Gospel could exalt Jesus as the true paschal Lamb, slain at the official time for slaughtering lambs for the Passover meal.

(2) *The significance of the foot-washing.* On the surface, at least, Jesus washed the disciples' feet as a lesson in humility. Laying aside his clothes and wearing a towel, as if he were a servant, he performed a menial task which Jewish masters were not even allowed to require of their slaves. But Jesus' words, "What I am

94]

doing you do not know now, but afterward you will understand" (v. 7), assure us that John saw a deeper, symbolic meaning in the washing. Some interpreters believe it referred to baptism. Verse 10 seems to endorse such a view; the word for "bathe" *(louein)* has cognates used for "baptize" in several New Testament references (e.g., Acts 22:16, 1 Cor. 6:11, Titus 3:5).

There is, however, a simpler interpretation. Only five days earlier, at another supper, Mary had anointed Jesus' feet in preparation for his death and burial (12:1–8). I suggested in the discussion of that passage that the customary place for anointing the body was the head, and that Mary anointed the feet as one might perfume the feet of a corpse. Suppose Jesus washed the feet of the disciples as a sign of their eventual martyrdom for the gospel. This would fit well with Origen's interpretation that the footwashing was related to preaching the gospel, and with the scripture

> How beautiful upon the mountains
> are the feet of him who brings
>   good tidings,
> who publishes peace, who brings
>   good tidings of good,
> who publishes salvation,
> who says to Zion, "Your God
>   reigns" (Isa. 52:7).

If it is indeed a correct interpretation, we might well include footwashing as a part of the ordination ceremony for those being commissioned to preach the Word.

(3) *The relationship of the washing to the betrayer.* The footwashing was obviously related to Judas' forthcoming act of betrayal. Jesus told the disciples, "You are clean, but not every one of you" (v. 10). John said this was because Jesus "knew who was to betray him" (v. 11). If our earlier interpretation is correct, that the footwashing was a preparation for dying for the gospel, then Judas would not have been "clean," even if his feet had been washed, for he would never preach the gospel.

The proof that the footwashing pertained to the disciples' coming deaths by martyrdom and not merely to humility is contained in verses 12–20. Jesus reclothed himself and took his place at the table with the disciples. He *first* spoke to them of what he had done as an example, that they too should be servants as he was a servant (vv.

15–16). Once more he exempted Judas from what he was saying, lest the disciples afterward think he did not know he harbored a betrayer in his midst. "I tell you this now," he said, "before it takes place, that when it does occur you may believe that I AM" (v. 19, P). Here again was the divine signature, the *egō eimi* without a modifier. *Then*, after talking about the exemplary nature of his act, Jesus added this important word about it: "Truly, truly, I say to you, he who receives any one whom I send receives me; and he who receives me receives him who sent me" (v. 20). In other words, the footwashing had to do with sending the disciples out. Jesus anointed their feet as a preparation for them to go out and preach— and subsequently to die for the gospel, as he was about to die.

Lord, prepare me to pay the price for the gospel of the kingdom you yourself were willing to pay. Let me say with Simon Peter, "Not my feet only, but also my hands and my head!" Let me give heart and soul and life for your kingdom's sake, and I shall be happy beyond words. For yours is the power and glory forever. Amen.

Week 7: Tuesday

John 13:21–30 The Drama of Betrayal

Jesus had emphasized to the disciples his foreknowledge of Judas' treachery. But the disciples themselves did not know, and were doubtless puzzled by his repeated references to a traitor in their midst. Thus, when Jesus openly said at the table, "I emphatically assure you, one of you will betray me" (v. 21, P), they looked around at once, wondering who the betrayer could be.

Jesus and the disciples were probably dining in the Roman fashion, lying on couches drawn up around three sides of the table. The disciple "whom Jesus loved"—probably John who wrote the Gospel—was "lying close to the breast of Jesus" (v. 23). As it was traditional to recline on the left elbow, John was undoubtedly on Jesus' right side, in a position where he could simply lay his head back to recline on Jesus' breast. Because John was so close and was a favorite disciple, Peter motioned to him to press the question with Jesus and learn the identity of the betrayer.

"Lord, who is it?" asked John (v. 25).

"The one to whom I give this morsel," said Jesus (v. 26, P). And he gave it to Judas.

The morsel may have been bread dipped in herbs or wine. Some interpreters have read into this a reference to communion, especially the form of communion known as intinction, in which the bread is dipped into the wine and the two are served together. This scene, in which Judas brazenly accepted the morsel from Jesus as a token of honor, would thus connect easily with Paul's warning in 1 Corinthians 11:27–29 that any one who eats the bread or drinks the cup of the Lord unworthily "eats and drinks judgment upon himself."

The drama at the table must have been intense as Jesus offered the morsel to Judas. Judas may still have been uncertain about whether to betray his master. (Verse 27 says that Satan entered into him only *after* he took the morsel.) If he had repented and confessed the treachery in his heart, his outcome might have been far different. But he received the morsel, ate it, and then determined to go ahead with his plans.

Judas may have been almost as close to Jesus at the table as John, for Jesus had handed him the morsel. As treasurer of the group, he probably held a place of importance, perhaps even on Jesus' left hand. It is likely, when Jesus spoke to him, that the others did not hear. "What you are going to do, do quickly," said Jesus (v. 27). And Judas went out.

Some of the disciples assumed that Jesus had sent him to acquire provisions for the Passover meal or had directed him to take some money to the poor, for he kept the money box.

There is an ominous note in John's words "and it was night" (v. 30). Jesus had come as the light of the world, and he was opposed by the darkness (1:4–5). Near the end of his public ministry, Jesus had warned: "Night comes" (9:4). "If any one walks in the night," he said, "he stumbles, because the light is not in him" (11:10). Now Judas had gone out into the darkness. Soon the darkness would appear to overcome the light.

Lord, my heart has always cried for Judas. Why should one be given to darkness and another to light? What is there in me, that I deserve your favor when another doesn't? Help me to be more worthy, that I may not betray the trust you have given me. Through Jesus, who suffers from all betrayal. Amen.

Week 7: Wednesday

John 13:31-38 Jesus' Farewell Speech

The farewell speech was a well-defined genre of Old Testament literature. It can be seen in the stories of such famous persons as Jacob (Gen. 47:29–49:33), Moses (the entire book of Deuteronomy), Joshua (Josh. 22–24), and David (1 Chron. 28–29). Certain features were always present in the farewell speech. They include: an announcement of the speaker's departure; comfort for those remaining behind; a review of the speaker's life and achievements; a reminder to keep the commandments of God; a call for unity and love among those left behind; a promise that the speaker's spirit will be close to those remaining; and a prayer for the ones remaining.

There can be little doubt that Jesus' long discourse at the Last Supper was intended as this kind of classical farewell speech. Jesus called the disciples "little children" (v. 33), as a man would speak to those he was leaving behind at death; it is the only time the term is used in the entire Fourth Gospel. He announced his departure (v. 33) and instructed the disciples to "love one another" (v. 34). And, in subsequent parts of the discourse, he would include all the other features of farewell speeches listed above.

"A new commandment," Jesus called his directive that the disciples love one another. Was it really a *new* commandment? Jewish scholars have often observed that the Old Testament likewise stressed the importance of love. When Jesus was asked to name the greatest commandment (Matt. 22:34–40; Mark 12:28–31), his response included Leviticus 19:18, that one is to love his neighbor as himself. Leviticus 19:34 even extended such love to foreigners: "The stranger who sojourns with you shall be to you as the native among you, and you shall love him as yourself; for you were strangers in the land of Egypt: I am the Lord your God."

Perhaps the "newness" in Jesus' commandment lay not in the commandment itself but in the motivational clause attached to it: "Love one another *as I have loved you*." In the Old Testament, the statement of the commandments began with the words "I am the Lord your God" (Exod. 20:2). The motivation to keep the commandments stemmed from the covenant relationship with God. Suppose, in Jesus' farewell discourse, he was citing a new, more intimate kind of motivation. He had described himself as the

98]

"beautiful shepherd" who lays down his life for the sheep (10:11). Now, in his final words to the disciples, he was saying, in effect, "Make this the basis of a new commandment: even as I have loved you, and given my life for you, love one another."

God had been more or less remote from the people of the Old Covenant. But he had come and stood in the midst of the people of the New Covenant. Now he was going to show them his love through the death of the Son. What stronger appeal could be made for their observing a commandment to love one another? People would know the disciples were followers of Jesus if they loved one another, for love was the distinguishing mark of his relationship to all of them.

Peter, characteristically, wanted to know where Jesus was going. He could not believe that the one who raised Lazarus from the grave should be speaking of his own death. Apparently he began to understand, however, for he swore he would lay down his life for Jesus. It was a case of the sheep's being willing to die for the shepherd.

But only the Shepherd's will was as good as his word. Peter would deny his relationship to Jesus three times before morning, and Jesus would give his life for the sheep on the following day.

Lord, I am gripped by Jesus' linking the love commandment to what he has done for me. How can I not love others, given such a reminder? Yet I do not. I forget what he has done, and, like Peter, deny him without thinking. Remind me, Lord. Keep me this day before the Cross. For his love's sake. Amen.

Week 7: Thursday

John 14:1–14 Words of Encouragement

The disciples were predictably distressed at Jesus' announcement of his departure. But his "comfortable teachings," many of them reminders of things he had said in his ministry, were drawn together as words of encouragement.

"Don't let your hearts be anxious," he said. "Believe in God and believe in me. There are rooms for all of you in my Father's house; otherwise, would I go to prepare a place for you?" (v. 1–2, P)

The word for rooms (*monē*) was customarily used for rest stops or temporary dwelling places, not for permanent homes. Early church fathers took this to signify a continuance of growth after death. The picture is of one's moving from level to level in understanding and of appropriating God's presence in the afterlife. Jesus goes ahead to prepare a place, and will come again to lead his disciples into these new realms of discipleship. If we remember the "beautiful shepherd" passage (10:1–18), we may imagine this as the shepherd's conducting the sheep into new, rich pasturelands.

(It is interesting, in the light of this passage, to recall the testimonies of many persons who have had "life after life" experiences—who were clinically dead and then returned to life with memories of the time while they were dead. Most of them have spoken of encountering a "guide" in the life beyond who would lead them into fresh understandings in their new environment. And, for many of them, this "guide" was Jesus.)

This time it was Thomas who led the way to further clarification of a saying of Jesus. "Lord," he said, "we do not know where you are going; how can we know the way?" (v. 5) Jesus' response to the question was another *egō eimi* saying, this time combining three great predicate modifiers: "I am the way, and the truth, and the life; no one comes to the Father, but by me" (v. 6).

"*I AM the way.*" Jesus had already identified himself as "the door of the sheep" (10:7). The disciples did not need to worry about finding their way to God when Jesus was gone. He was the way, and, as long as they remained in him and his teachings, they would have no trouble arriving at their spiritual home.

"*I AM the truth.*" Rabbis were constantly trying to discover truth and impart it to their followers. Jesus did not have to search for truth. He was the eternal Word, the Wisdom of God in the flesh, the Light that enlightens everyone who comes into the world. Hence he could say, without equivocation, "I AM the truth."

"*I AM the life.*" The entire Gospel has been about life. Jesus has identified himself as "the water of life" and "the bread of life." Those who drink the water he gives them will never thirst (4:14); those who eat his bread will never hunger (6:35). Any who believe in him will not perish, but will have eternal life (3:16). The disciples would not only have life in the world to come; in Jesus, they had it already, for he *was* the life.

What did Jesus mean, "No one comes to the Father, but by me"? Is this a declaration of exclusivism, a way of saying there is absolutely no salvation outside the Christian faith? Jesus had all along identified himself as the Son of the Father, who did the works of the Father (see especially 5:17, 19–24). He and the Father, he said, were one. Therefore, to come to the Father was to come to the Son. And, conversely, to come to the Son was to come to the Father. "If you had known me, you would have known my Father also; henceforth you know him and have seen him" (v. 7).

Philip still did not understand. "Show us the Father," he asked. "Have I been with you so long," replied Jesus, "and you don't understand? If you have seen me, you have seen the Father. You have beheld the works I do. They are not my works, but the Father's. Don't you see? I am the very extension of the Father. He is in me and I am in him" (vv. 9–10, P).

There was more. Not only was Jesus in the Father, so that he did the Father's works, but the disciples, who were in Jesus, would also do the Father's works. The extraordinary power of the Creator would flow from them as it had flowed from the Son. Anything they asked *in his name* would be done.

"In my name." Many of our prayers have come to be signed "in Jesus' name." It is not that there is magic in the formula, but that there is power in the reality to which it attests. It speaks of our being in communion with the One whose name we employ, so that we signify, by speaking his name, that we are extensions of his work in the world. And there is nothing in the world, as the raising of Lazarus demonstrated, that can resist the power of the Son and the Father!

> *Heavenly Father, I am prone to wish power for my own sake, and to pray in Jesus' name without really dwelling in his spirit. What a dangerous thing it is to pray in his name if I really mean it; then I am like a toy sailboat swept out to sea on a bottomless tide! Help me to pray the phrase and to mean it—whatever the cost. Amen.*

Week 7: Friday

John 14:15–24   Children of the Covenant

"A new commandment I give to you, that you love one another," Jesus said; "even as I have loved you, that you also love one another" (13:34). Now he says, "If you love me, you will keep my commandments" (14:15). Both verses suggest that we are dealing in this passage with a new covenant situation. In the Old Testament, the Jews identified themselves with God by keeping his commandments; Jesus expects his followers to identify with him the same way.

Covenant-keeping followers will be given a special "Spirit of truth" as a counselor and guide, and the Spirit will dwell in them. Jesus calls the Spirit *"another* Paraclete" (or "counselor"), suggesting that he himself has been the first. This Paraclete will help them to understand all that has happened. As we shall see, the notion of the second Paraclete is not fully developed, as the doctrine of the Trinity would be at a later date, but appears to be a way of saying that the Spirit of the Father and the Son will be with them. "I will not leave you desolate," says Jesus; "I will come to you" (v. 18). The Jerusalem Bible and The Living Bible translate more literally: "I will not leave you orphans" (Greek *orphanous*). Earlier, Jesus called the disciples "little children" (13:33); now he promises not to forsake them as children with no leadership or provision.

What does it mean that Jesus will come to them? Is this the *parousia*, or Second Coming? Possibly so, but not as the Synoptic Gospels interpret the Second Coming. John is more inclined to think of Jesus' return as his spiritual reappearance to the disciples after his resurrection. Soon the world will not see him; but the disciples will see him (v. 19). Then they will know that he is in the Father (v. 20), and he will show himself to them (v. 21). Not only that, but both Jesus and the Father will come and make their home with the disciples (v. 23).

The word for "home" in verse 23 is the same word used in verse 2, "In my Father's house are many homes" (or "dwelling-places"). The idea is circular, to express the central truth of the new covenant. God will dwell with his children and they will dwell with him. And the disciples will understand all these things later, after the resurrection has occurred.

O Lord, these matters are hard to understand unless one has felt them. Help me to feel them more deeply and certainly from day to day, and to lead others to experience them too, that we may dwell together with you in perfect unity. Through him who gave his life that we might know you as you are. Amen.

Week 7: Saturday

John 14:25–31   The Great Bequest

This passage concludes the first section of Jesus' farewell speech, and Jesus emphasizes his departure in verse 25 ("These things I have spoken to you, while I am still with you") and verse 30 ("I will no longer talk much with you").

Again he speaks of the Paraclete, this time using the full phrase "the Holy Spirit." The Father will send the Holy Spirit "in my name," says Jesus, reminding us of the phrase in verse 13 ("Whatever you ask in my name, I will do it") and once more emphasizing the unity theme of the entire discourse. The Spirit's work will be to continue teaching the disciples and to cause them to remember all of Jesus' words and understand them in the light of what transpires. (Cf. 13:7, "What I am doing you do not know now, but afterward you will understand.")

Jesus then makes his final bequest to the disciples—his peace (v. 27). Most persons about to die make parting gifts to those closest to them. Jesus is an itinerant rabbi, with nothing of great worldly value to leave behind. But he gives the disciples a priceless inheritance—his blessing of fullness. In Jewish thought, the word "peace" (Hebrew *shalom*) meant more than the absence of conflict; it meant fullness of being. Jesus knew it was a special gift: "not as the world gives do I give to you" (v. 27). And peace, along with grace, was to become a part of the standard Christian greeting after Jesus' death and resurrection. It is a Christian's most precious possession, something, as Paul said, that passes all ordinary understanding (Phil. 4:7).

In further consolation for what is to happen, Jesus tells the disciples that if they only understood his love and their union with him, they would be glad he is going to the Father, for the Father is greater than he (v. 28). This is not a statement about unequal powers within the Trinity, any more than the talk of a Paraclete was a full-grown trinitarian statement. Jesus simply means that he is returning to the One who sent him, who, in the sense of being the originating parent, always takes precedence. Later, Paul will reflect the same attitude of rejoicing about going to the Father and the Son: "For to me to live is Christ, and to die is gain. If it is to be life

[103

in the flesh, that means fruitful labor for me. Yet which I shall choose I cannot tell. I am hard pressed between the two. My desire is to depart and be with Christ, for that is far better" (Phil. 1:21–23).

The ruler of this world, says Jesus, does not really have the power he will appear to have. Evil will seem to control everything—even the destiny of the one who is the Light of the World and the Beautiful Shepherd. But the control is an illusion. Jesus submits to death not at Satan's command but at the Father's, in order that the world may understand the nature of true obedience—or, as Jesus puts it, "so that the world may know that I love the Father" (v. 31).

Finally, Jesus bids the disciples to rise and go out with him, terminating this part of the discourse. Some interpreters suggest that the second part—chapters fifteen and sixteen—occurs on the way to Gethsemane, and that the image of the vine and the branches in 15:1–11 was occasioned by their passing either some vines or a pile of dead branches pruned away from the vines. Others believe that the entire discourse took place in the upper room and the command to rise and go out was merely a displaced instruction. Either way, the sentence marks a clear division in the final discourse.

In the storms of life, O Christ, give me your peace and I shall be content. Nothing matters as much as your presence. Teach me to be still and know you, that I may no longer fear the wind and the waves. For you are the Lord of all. Amen.

WEEK 8

Week 8: Sunday

John 15:1-11 The Vine and the Branches

Here is another *egō eimi* passage, with Jesus this time using the grapevine as an image of his life and work. We recall that his images often reflected the failure of Israel and his own supplanting of old traditions. Thus, the well of Jacob was insufficient, but Jesus was the giver of "living water" (4:7-15); the manna of Moses was unfilling, but Jesus was "the bread of life" (6:25-35); the special candles lit at the Feast of Tabernacles illuminated the city of Jerusalem, but Jesus was "the light of the world" (8:12); the shepherds of Israel cared only for their own comfort and prosperity, but Jesus was "the beautiful shepherd" who laid down his life for the sheep (10:11-15).

By calling himself "the true vine" or "the real vine," Jesus was reflecting again on the failure of national religion in Israel. There are many references in the Old Testament to Israel as a vineyard (cf. Isa. 5:1-7, 27:2-6; Jer. 5:10, 12:10-11) or as a vine (cf. Ps. 80:8-11; Ezek. 17:1-10). Most of these references are negative; they deal with Israel's breaking of her covenant with God and God's consequent destruction of the vineyard or the vine. Jesus, by contrast with the unfaithful nation, was the genuine stock of the vineyard, the one for whom God cared and who would bear fruit for the great vinedresser.

Therefore it was important that the disciples remain in him, and not seek their life in another vine or another vineyard. This was a clear word to Christian Jews facing expulsion from the synagogues. Only by keeping their attachment to Jesus would they have life. Away from him, they would become like the branches pruned from the trunk and thrown away to wither.

There is even an ominous note for those who do remain in Jesus but bear no fruit. They too will be cut away and destroyed, so that they do not inhibit the better branches from bearing fruit. Judas, we assume, was thus removed. The other disciples had been made clean (that is, in the way fruit-bearing branches were trimmed to give more nourishment to the fruit) by "the word" Jesus had spoken to them. The word was the *logos* of chapter one—the Wisdom of God addressed to the disciples through Jesus' teachings.

The image of the vine and the branches fits beautifully with the entire theme of unity in the farewell discourse. Over and over, Jesus stressed the importance of remaining in him as he remained in the Father, and drawing on his love as he drew on the Father's love. If the disciples only continued in him, they would have Jesus' joy in them—the creative excitement of knowing they were at the center of God's will for human life—and their joy would be full (v. 11).

Lord, help me to remain in you and follow your commandment to love others as you have loved me, that I may shout with joy at what I see and know. For yours is the life for ever and ever. Amen.

Week 8: Monday

John 15:12–17 The Greatest Motivation of All

"No longer do I call you servants," said Jesus, "for the servant does not know what his master is doing; but I have called you friends"—the Greek is *beloved* or *loved ones*—"for all that I have heard from my Father I have made known to you" (v. 15).

What a touching scene this is—a man about to die, giving his farewell discourse, and saying to his servants, the menials who have tended to the basic needs of his life, "You are no longer my servants, you are my dearly prized friends, my loved ones"! What a sense of unity it implies! And what consequences it would have in the disciples' lives!

We hear a lot today about motivation. Firms search for ways of motivating employees. Teachers try to motivate students. Advertising agencies wish to motivate consumers. But here is the greatest example of motivation in the world.

Jesus was the incarnate Wisdom of God, the eternal Son, the King of Glory. Yet he loved his disciples with such intense passion that he laid down his life for them and called them his dearly beloved friends. "You didn't choose to follow me," he said, "but I chose you, because I knew you would be fruitful for the Father. Now, continue in my love by walking in the way I have shown you, and love one another in the way you see me loving you, and the Father will care for all your needs, in my name" (vv. 16–17, P).

Is it any wonder the disciples went to the ends of the earth, suffered in prisons, or died on crosses for him? Who wouldn't have done the same?

In the stillness, O Christ, I know that you have loved me as you did your first disciples. The words you said to them are spoken to me as well. How can I love you, Lord? Let me withhold nothing of myself, but give you everything. For you have given all for me. Amen.

Week 8: Tuesday

John 15:18–16:4a   The World's Hatred for the Disciples

If Jesus had testified to the disciples of his love for them, he had also to warn them of the world's hatred for them. The hatred would stem from the fact that they bore his name and were identified with the works he did. After all, he had many times revealed himself as the I AM of God—the one whose presence makes all earthly institutions appear shabby by comparison. And those who had anything to uphold or protect in those institutions would be innately opposed to him, as the darkness is opposed to the light.

"The Jews" would hate the Christians because Christ threatened their authority in religious matters. The Romans would hate them because they worshiped Jesus instead of Caesar. Jesus said he was hated to fulfill the word of Psalm 35:19 and Psalm 69:4 about "those who hate me without cause." From a spiritual perspective, neither "the Jews" nor the Romans had just cause to hate him. But the perfidious thing about hate is always its baselessness and ridiculousness. "To understand everything," said Voltaire, "is to forgive everything." Had "the Jews" and Romans only understood, they would have loved instead of hated.

The Paraclete, said Jesus, would help to teach the disciples about these things and would bear witness to him. There would be times when they would need that witness, lest they think they had followed a madman and bargained poorly with their souls.

As we have noted all along, the Fourth Gospel was written primarily to encourage Christian Jews being put out of synagogues. In 16:1–14, Jesus said that the main purpose of his farewell speech was to prevent their falling away from the faith. He knew they would be expelled from the synagogues. Worse, the time would come when some Jews would even seek their deaths as worship or service to God (the Greek *latreia* meant both "worship" and "service"). But they were to remain in him, as branches in the true vine, and he and the Father would care for them and give them eternal life.

Lord, I have seldom felt persecuted for my faith. Does this mean that my faith has not been radical enough to provoke the fear and envy of others? Help me to ponder this question today and face its implications in my daily life. For your name's sake. Amen.

Week 8: Wednesday

John 16:4b–15 The Role of the Spirit

It was not necessary, as long as Jesus was with the disciples, that he tell them all the things he put into his farewell speech. Before leaving them, however, he wished them to be conscious of these matters.

Did hearing them make the disciples sad? It shouldn't, because

Jesus' going to the Father would be to their advantage. He would send the other counselor of whom he had spoken (14:16) and the counselor would convict the world of its sin, injustice, and wrongdoing (v. 8).

The Greek words I have translated as "to convict" have a variety of meanings. They can mean "expose," "bring to light," "correct," or even "punish." The King James or Authorized Version reads "reprove"; the Revised Standard Version and Living Bible, "convince"; and the New English Bible, "confute." The Jerusalem Bible translation of the entire passage is interesting:

> And when he comes,
> he will show the world how wrong it was,
> about sin,
> and about who was in the right,
> and about judgment (v. 8).

The idea is that the Spirit would set everything in a new perspective, so that many would understand that Jesus was not a self-willed impostor but the true Son of God. They would know that they sinned in not believing in Jesus; that they were unrighteous, because the Son of righteousness was killed and left in their midst; and that they were under judgment, because the prince of this world, their ruler, had been judged.

The Spirit would also reveal many things to the disciples they could not presently bear—either because there was too much for them to remember or because the sayings would tax their understanding. The Spirit's revelations would come as they needed them. "Whatever he hears he will speak" (v. 13) probably refers to the divine council—the Spirit repeats to the disciples what he has heard in the presence of the Father and the Son. "He will declare to you the things that are to come" (v. 13) does not mean that the Spirit predicts the future but that he interprets whatever happens. The verb translated "declare" means "to reannounce" or "republish," as if the Spirit's function is to remind the disciples of what has already been declared and help them see its relationship to everything occurring in the present. He will glorify Jesus by bringing to mind everything belonging to the Son.

Teach me, O Spirit, to listen to you about Jesus and the world. Help me to understand—to feel deeply—the things that matter about his incarnation and what it means to the world, that I may be your servant in all things. Through him who walked the land and sailed the sea. Amen.

Week 8: Thursday

John 16:16–24   The Joy Beyond the Pain

"A little while, and you will see me no more; again a little while, and you will see me" (v. 16). What did Jesus mean by these words? The disciples were rightly puzzled. Looking back, we can easily see what was meant by the first statement; it referred to Jesus' impending death. But did the second statement refer to his reappearance after the resurrection, to a second coming at some future time, or to the disciples' reunion with Jesus in the afterlife?

Jesus' analogy in verses 21–22, of the woman who goes through anguish in giving birth and then forgets the anguish in her joy for the child, almost certainly interprets the words as applying to his post-resurrection appearances to the disciples. They would suffer great pain at the time of the crucifixion, but it would be forgotten in their ecstasy at seeing him afterward.

"So you have sorrow now, but I will see you again and your hearts will rejoice, and no one will take your joy from you" (v. 22).

Again, Jesus spoke to the disciples of asking "in my name." They had not done this before, he said; in the future, they should do it, and see how full their joy was. He was not giving them the key to self-indulgence, so they could ask indiscriminately for whatever they wished. His words must be interpreted in light of the entire discourse and its emphasis on unity—on being in him and in the Father. A person in that intimate spiritual relationship does not desire things for the self. He or she wishes what the Father and Son wish—the healing of cripples, the sight of the blind, the raising of the dead, the love of all people for one another. "Ask these things in my name," Jesus was saying to the disciples, "and you will have what you ask, and your joy will overflow."

Lord, I know your words were not meant for the disciples alone, but for all followers. I want to be part of the unity you described, so that my desires are transformed by your love and your truth. Help me to will the things you will, and to will them so devotedly that I may see them come to pass. For your name's sake. Amen.

Week 8: Friday

John 16:25–33   A New Stage of Relationship

"I have said this to you in figures," said Jesus. To what does "this" refer? To the foregoing verse, which speaks of asking in Jesus' name and having joy? To the whole final discourse? Or to Jesus' entire ministry, in which he has characterized himself by such figures of speech as "the bread of life," "the light of the world," and "the beautiful shepherd"?

Perhaps it does not matter, as Jesus spoke in figures throughout his relationship with the disciples. The important thing is that their relationship was about to transcend all figures and become so intimate that it would not need language at all. Jesus would be in their hearts, speaking the language of the heart, and assuring them directly of the Father's love.

Jesus would no longer pray to the Father for them. Being in the Son and Father, they would ask what they wished in the Son's name—"for the Father himself loves you, because you have loved me and have believed that I came from the Father" (v. 27).

Jesus had come from the Father to do the Father's work, and he was going back to the Father now that the work was done. Suddenly the disciples seemed to understand. "Now we know that you know all things, and need none to question you; by this we believe that you came from God" (v. 30). The phrase "need none to question you" is a puzzling one. It may refer to the way the disciples and others constantly questioned Jesus in order that he could give them the truth; now, as Spirit, he would impart truth in another way, directly and without need of a rabbinical structure.

Again Jesus warned the disciples of difficult times to come. They would be scattered as sheep without their shepherd. Yet they were not to be concerned about the shepherd. God would not leave him alone. However desolate he might appear to be, the Father was with him. Luke would picture him, in the final moments of life, saying, "Father, into thy hands I commit my spirit" (23:46). There was no reason for John to report these words; Jesus had told the disciples many times of his relationship to the Father; they knew he would not be abandoned.

Jesus predicted the disciples' scattering (this may also have been a reference to the Dispersion throughout the Empire) and told of his being with the Father to assure them of their continued blessing in him and the Father. The world might hate them and give them enormous difficulty, but Jesus would continue to give them peace and joy, for he had overcome the world.

The tense of the last verb suggests that his overcoming did not even await the resurrection. His "hour" had come, and God was glorifying him through everything that transpired—even his trial and death!

Lord, I am grateful for the figures that have taught me how to see you. It is wonderful to picture you as light and bread, shepherd and true vine. Yet the most thrilling moments of all are those when I annihilate all thought and feel you warm and strong as a presence without images or figures at all. Then I know you as the disciples did, and understand your triumph over the world. Give me such a moment now, Lord, for your name's sake. Amen.

Week 8: Saturday

John 17:1–5   Jesus' Great Pastoral Prayer

This is the longest prayer by Jesus recorded in the Gospels. It extends through the entire chapter. Structurally, it is part of the farewell speech begun near the end of chapter thirteen. Farewell speeches in the Old Testament frequently included a prayer for those being left behind, and it was natural for Jesus to follow the pattern.

John, unlike the Synoptic Gospels, includes no prayer of Jesus in Gethsemane—that, if it be the Father's will, the cup might pass from him. The Jesus of the Fourth Gospel is far more triumphant than the Jesus of the Synoptics. He does not agonize over the cross. Instead, he sees the cross as his hour of glory, when he will return to the Father. God has given him "power over all flesh" (v. 2); he is already the cosmic Christ. Therefore the prayer he offers is a great pastoral prayer—the prayer of the "beautiful shepherd" for his sheep.

The prayer is divided into three sections. First, Jesus addresses the Father and speaks of the hour of his glory (vv. 1–5). Then he prays for the disciples (vv. 6–19). Finally, he prays for all who are to become followers in the years ahead (vv. 20–26). Someone has observed that the prayer thus resembles one offered by Aaron, the high priest, in Leviticus 16:11–17. Aaron first prayed for himself, then for his priestly family, and finally for the whole people. John may well have been conscious of these parallels when he set down the prayer of Jesus, for, as Aaron was the great high priest of the old covenant, Jesus was the great high priest of the new!

Jesus begins the prayer by addressing the Father and asking for his glorification. Glory is a quality of Godhood. It emanates from God in the same way the energy of our solar system emanates from the sun. As the Son of God, Jesus had shared in that glory before coming into the world. Now, returning to the Father, he asks to share in it once more.

Seeing the Son's glory enables people to have eternal life. "This is eternal life," says Jesus, "that they know thee the only true God, and Jesus Christ whom thou has sent" (v. 3). *Knowing*, in the Hebrew world view, meant more than cerebral awareness; it meant *participation* in what was known. To know something was to be intimately involved with it. Thus, to know Jesus was to have one's destiny entwined with his—to be one with him and the Father.

We are prone, after centuries of emphasis on salvation through Jesus' death on the cross, to exalt that aspect of his work. But John saw the importance of the post-resurrection state of Jesus—of his triumph over the world and return to the bosom of the Father. John did not neglect a detailed account of the Passion; he simply emphasized the eternal nature of Christ and the completion of his work by rejoining the Father in glory.

The Orthodox Church, which has followed John's Gospel more closely than the Synoptics, to this day retains a strong sense of resurrection and triumphalism in its worship. The center of its services is the exalted Christ, not the humble Jesus of Galilee. The figure most often found in its church buildings is the Pantocrator Christ—the glorified Messiah with arms outstretched over the world. One can almost hear him say, when viewing it, "Be of good cheer, I have overcome the world" (16:33).

Lord, as the moon possesses no glory of its own, but reflects the brilliance of the burning sun, help me in my darkness to receive the glory of your presence and reflect it to those who dwell in a land of shadows; for yours is the kingdom and the power and the glory forever. Amen.

WEEK 9

Week 9: Sunday

John 17:6–19   The Prayer for the Disciples

In some ways, this section of Jesus' great pastoral prayer seems to have been uttered not before Jesus' death but after his resurrection—indeed, many years later. Jesus speaks of the disciples' having kept God's word (v. 6) and having been hated by the world (v. 14). At the time of the prayer's setting, between the Last Supper and the visit to Gethsemane, these things can hardly have come to pass. In fact, Jesus has only moments earlier (15:18–27) warned the disciples that they will be hated, and has promised them the Holy Spirit for encouragement. We can but suppose that John, with the liberty of a creative editor, has written the prayer not only as it applied to the disciples when Jesus prayed it but as it came to apply to them and other disciples years after Jesus' return to the Father.

"I manifested thy name," says Jesus, "to the men whom thou gavest me out of the world" (v. 6). Was this Jesus' mission, to reveal God's name? A name, among the Hebrews, was supposed to contain the very essence of a person. Yahweh, the holiest name of God, was for that reason not lightly spoken. The people never uttered it in common speech. Only the high priest was allowed to speak it—and then only on the Day of Atonement. Jesus had made his disciples familiar with God's name and personality—something unheard of among ordinary people.

God's name, in the Fourth Gospel, may be related to Jesus' frequent use of the phrase *egō eimi*—I AM. It did correspond to God's giving the name Yahweh to himself in speaking to Moses at the burning bush, for Yahweh meant I AM. Jesus not only gave the disciples the holy name, he coupled it with images that revealed the holy personality. I AM was the bread of life (6:35), the light of the world (8:12), the door of the sheep (10:7), the beautiful shepherd (10:14), the resurrection and the life (11:25), the true vine (15:1), the way, the truth, and the life (14:6). He came walking on the stormy sea in the dark of night (6:20). He made the crippled spring up (5:2–9), the blind see (9:1–12), and the dead live (11:1–44). Surely the disciples were overwhelmed by Jesus' revelation of the "name" of God. It is no wonder they believed he was sent from the Father.

Like the great shepherd he is, Jesus has kept the disciples given to him—all except Judas, "the son of perdition." Now, going away from them, he prays for their continued unity in him and the Father. He does not ask that they too be taken out of the world— only that they be kept from the evil one while they are in the world.

"As thou didst send me into the world," says Jesus, "so I have sent them into the world" (v. 18). Against the background of the entire Gospel that has preceded it, this is a remarkable statement. The Father sent the Son into the world to do his works. He and the Son were one in everything. At the end of his mission, the Son went back to the glory of the Father. It will be the same for the disciples. They will take up the works of the Son. They will be one with him in everything. And, finally, they will join him in glory, leaving yet more disciples to do the works of the Son and the Father.

What a name you have revealed to us, O Lord. It is a name of music and poetry, a name of life and love and joy, a name surpassing every name. Help me to live daily in its great mystery, until my life is fully converted to your way, and I am yours for ever and ever. Amen.

Week 9: Monday

John 17:20–26   A Prayer for Future Believers

Jesus' great pastoral prayer finally includes all of those who would come to believe in him through the ministry of the disciples. It is essentially the prayer offered for the disciples themselves—that they may all be one with him and the Father.

We can imagine how encouraging this prayer was to the Jewish Christians who were being put out of their synagogues and separated from the Jewish communities. They must have read the words again and again, drawing hope and joy from the thoughts of being in Christ.

In verse 24, Jesus expresses a desire for both his present and future followers to be with him in the life after the resurrection, so they can behold the glory he had with the Father before the creation of the world. As believers, they already know something of this glory. But in the life beyond death they will be in the presence of eternal Wisdom in all its glory, with no barriers to their understanding.

Phillips Brooks once spoke of the division between this life and the next as a curtain. Sometimes, he said, we see the curtain tremble—especially if a loved one has recently gone beyond. It is enough to remind us of the life on the other side. But when we die we ourselves pass beyond the curtain, and nothing will then inhibit us from seeing and knowing all things.

Jesus was anxious for his followers to join him beyond the curtain. Then they would see all they had believed and hoped, given form in the heavenly world. The "name" Jesus had revealed to them—that of the great I AM himself—would be fulfilled in the unspeakable presence to which it alluded. The love with which they had been loved would see them safely home to the bosom of the Father, who would then be "all in all."

I can live my life more fully, Lord, knowing that its ultimate destiny is to dwell with you forever. Let my words and deeds remind others of this knowledge, that they too may come to know you and live in your love. For your kingdom's sake. Amen.

Week 9: Tuesday

John 18:1–12   Jesus Taken Captive

Having given his farewell speech and prayer, Jesus went with the disciples to the garden where he often met with them. Luke also said it was Jesus' "custom" to go there (22:39), but John alone calls the place a garden. The Synoptics all speak only of "the Mount of Olives" and "a place called Gethsemane." Perhaps John wished to emphasize the symbolism of the place, and relate it to the garden where Adam and Eve first sinned against God.

To reach the garden, Jesus and the disciples crossed the little brook Kidron. It was called "winter-flowing Kidron" because it was a mere wadi, or stream bed, and was dry except at the time of the late winter rains, in February and March. John may have mentioned the Kidron for two reasons. One is prophetic: in 1 Kings 2:37, Solomon warned Shimei, "On the day you go forth, and cross the brook Kidron, know for certain that you shall die." The other reason is prophetic too, but in a different way: during Passover, the brook flowed with the blood of lambs slain at the temple.

Because Jesus was accustomed to going with his disciples to the garden, Judas knew where to find him, and came leading "a band of soldiers and some officers from the chief priests and the Pharisees" (v. 3). The word for "band," literally, is "cohort." A cohort was six hundred Roman soldiers. It seems unlikely that Pilate would have dispatched so many men to arrest Jesus; therefore the translators have preferred a less precise term. John's is the only Gospel involving the Romans in Jesus' arrest; in the other Gospels, it is the temple guard that comes. Some interpreters think John may have been universalizing Jesus' enemies in this way—and underlining what Jesus said to the disciples about being hated by "the world" (15:18). The other Gospels, however, may have wished to downplay the Roman part in the arrest to avoid difficulties with the government, and John's account may be the more accurate one.

The soldiers and police came with "lanterns and torches and weapons." John probably liked this touch in his narrative, for it emphasized again the darkness out of which they came to Jesus, who was the light of the world. Their weapons would have been clubs and swords, and possibly spears. One can imagine the scene, as they swarmed over the hillside of the Mount of Olives, their lanterns and torches forming winding paths of light among the rocks and olive trees and grape vines, and their armor clinking audibly in the night.

In the Synoptic accounts, Judas came forward to Jesus and identified him for the police. Here, Jesus is in complete command, as we would expect him to be in John's Gospel; "knowing all that would befall him," he stepped forward to the searchers and said, "Whom do you seek?" "Jesus of Nazareth," they replied. "I am he," said Jesus. Literally, in the Greek, the words were *egō eimi*—I AM. The searchers recoiled and fell to the ground. Some suppose this was because Jesus had uttered the name of God—the name no one but the high priest was allowed to speak. It is unlikely that a cohort of Roman soldiers would have been so affected by the name of a Hebrew deity unknown to them. Instead, it was probably Jesus' personal bearing that at first frightened and intimidated them— though we cannot be sure it was not the other.

Again Jesus asked whom they sought. It was as if he did so to revive them, to start up the drama again. This time, when they told him whom they sought, he said once more that it was he, but that they should let his disciples go. "This," says John, "was to fulfill the word which he had spoken, 'Of those whom thou gavest me I lost not one'" (v. 9).

John repeatedly emphasizes Jesus' not losing any disciples (6:39; 10:38; 17:12); in 17:12, he has Jesus excepting Judas, for Judas was foreordained to be lost. This accent on the security of those in Jesus was surely for the benefit of Jewish Christians having to choose between Christ and the synagogue. The synagogue was willing to turn them out, but Jesus would never lose those whom God had given him.

Simon Peter, who in all the Gospels has a reputation for impetuousness, drew a sword and struck the slave of the high priest, Malchus, cutting off part of his ear. The word for ear, *ōtarion*, suggests an earlobe, not the entire ear. As Judas was in league with the high priest, he was probably close to the high priest's slave, together with those who commanded the soldiers and police. Peter was most likely striking into the midst of the enemy leadership.

But again Jesus was in command. His hour had come and he was ready to drink the cup his Father gave him. In the Synoptic accounts, he prayed in the garden for the cup to pass. Here, however, he seems eager for the cross to come, that he may join the Father in glory. So he tells Peter to put up the sword, and permits the soldiers and police to bind him and take him away.

Lord, this was a dramatic encounter, when you faced your enemies and did not use your great power to overcome them. Teach me your calmness of soul before those who would be my enemies, that I may not be disturbed by the evil of the world. For you are my strength and my redeemer. Amen.

Week 9: Wednesday

John 18:13–18   The Infidelity of Peter

Bound by the soldiers and police, Jesus was taken to the home of Caiaphas, the high priest. Caiaphas's aged father-in-law Annas, who had been high priest a few years earlier and still wielded much political force among the Jews, was also there. Some historiographers believe that Caiaphas' and Annas' homes adjoined one another, possibly with this infamous courtyard between them.

The focus is temporarily turned not on Jesus but on Peter, who in the garden had offered resistance to the soldiers and police and then followed the crowd to Caiaphas' house when Jesus was brought there. There is a mystery disciple in the passage, whose presence gained entrance for Peter into the high priest's courtyard. He was "known to the high priest," says John, and "entered the court of the high priest along with Jesus" (v. 15). Speculation about the mystery disciple's identity has centered principally on three persons.

Some think it was the beloved disciple John, who consistently hesitated to mention his own name in the Gospel. If it was not John, then why does the account fail to identify the disciple? The author surely knew the man's name, for he even had the name of the unfortunate slave whose ear was severed in the garden.

Other commentators suggest that the unnamed disciple was Nicodemus, who is pictured in 19:39 coming with spices and ointments to anoint Jesus' body for burial. Nicodemus was apparently a crypto-disciple, and would have been well known in

Caiaphas' house, so that he could have gained entrance for Peter. But why would John have failed to name him? He would not have been more endangered by identification here than in chapter twenty.

The third possibility is that the unknown disciple was Judas. Judas certainly was known to the high priest, having negotiated with him for the betrayal of Jesus, and would almost surely have followed with the soldiers and police he had led to the garden. The maid at the gate knew that the mystery figure was a disciple, for she asked Peter if he was also a disciple. Peter's denial indicates that it was not safe to admit to discipleship, which means that John could not have gone there freely. Judas could, for he had sold out his master. But would he have helped Peter gain entrance?

The Gospel is not concerned with answering our questions about this unidentified person. Its entire focus is on Peter and his act of infidelity. No story in the annals of discipleship was more important to the distraught Jewish Christians than this one. If Peter could fluctuate so greatly in a matter of hours, from single-handedly attacking the soldiers to denying that he was a follower of Jesus, then the falling away of other Christians was an understandable act of human frailty. And if Peter could be restored to fellowship—even to leadership—then there was always hope for those who had denied Christ in the synagogues, that they could be forgiven and rejoined to the fledgling Christian community.

> *Lord, this is my hope too. How often I deny you in my self-centeredness, my forgetfulness of others, and my doubts and fears. I am not worthy to be called your follower. Yet you forgive me and anoint me again with your Spirit and send me forth to do your bidding. Let me not fail you today, I pray, but live honestly and openly for you, for my friends' and family's sake. Amen.*

Week 9: Thursday

John 18:19–24 Jesus before Annas

There is apparent confusion in this passage about who interrogated Jesus. We were told in verse 13 that Jesus was led to Annas, the father-in-law of Caiaphas, and are informed in verse 24, when the interrogation was ended, that Annas "sent him bound to Caiaphas the high priest." But verse 19 says "the *high priest* then questioned Jesus about his disciples and his teaching"—before he was sent to Caiaphas. It seems impossible to separate the tangle, further complicated in verse 28, where we are told that Jesus was led from the house of Caiaphas to the praetorium, without any word of his being questioned there.

But some light is shed on the matter by Acts 4:6, which refers to "Annas the high priest and Caiaphas and John and Alexander, and all who were of the high-priestly family." Annas was clearly the head of a priestly dynasty. In all, he had five sons who became high priests. Caiaphas held the office in the year of Jesus' trial and crucifixion. But always it was Annas—the crafty, powerful patriarch of the family—who took precedence in important matters. For this reason, he continued to be known as the high priest even while his sons were in office.

It is probable, therefore, that the high priest referred to in verse 19 was Annas. The old patriarch himself was up in the middle of the night, questioning Jesus about "his disciples and his teaching."

Persons brought before the powerful old priest would normally have cowered and answered his questions submissively. Jesus radiated confidence and self-possession. "I have not conducted my ministry in secret," he said in effect. "Why am I being dealt with secretly here?" His demand that others be asked about him was tantamount to requesting an open trial.

One of the temple police, unaccustomed to such boldness before the old man, struck Jesus in the face and asked, "Is that how you answer the high priest?" (v. 22) In the Synoptic Gospels, Jesus received even worse treatment: he was spit upon, blindfolded, and made to prophesy who hit him (Matt. 26:67–68; Mark 14:65; Luke 22:63–64). John would surely have been troubled to report such indignities to the eternal Word; a slap in the face was all he would allow himself to describe.

Not even a blow in the face, however, curbed Jesus' spirit. "If I was wrong," he said, "then take me to trial. If I was not, then why am I struck?" (v. 23, P).

Annas was surely not satisfied by Jesus' answers, but could do nothing else. So he sent him to his son Caiaphas—either in another part of the house or in a house adjoining. His son was now officially the high priest—*he* would have to deal with Jesus.

Lord, it is sad that religious leaders can be part of the web of evil and darkness in the world. I suppose any of us can, even without intending to. Teach me to live in such daily humility before you that I may never offend you while thinking I am performing my duty. For yours is a name above every name, both in heaven and on earth. Amen.

Week 9: Friday

John 18:25–27   Afraid in the Courtyard

For the second time, John mentions that Peter was warming himself at the charcoal fire in the courtyard of the high priest (vv. 18 and 25). Jerusalem is half a mile above sea level, and the spring nights are often quite chilly. The confrontation between Annas and Jesus may have required an hour or more, for Annas probably spent time conferring with his associates about what should be done with the Nazarene. Peter, having nothing to do but wait in the courtyard, undoubtedly grew cold and moved to the fireside.

We can imagine what was going through his head. Jesus had been marched off as a captive. The longer he was gone, the more frightened Peter became. Was Jesus less powerful than he had believed? Why didn't he strike his enemies a mortal blow and walk out of the high priest's house? The constant movement of soldiers and police in the courtyard must have been unnerving to an outsider.

The girl who watched the gate had asked Peter if he was a disciple of Jesus and he denied it (v. 17). Now, when others standing about the fire thought they recognized him, he denied it again. Then one of the servants of the high priest, studying Peter's face in the firelight, decided Peter must be the man who had attacked his cousin in the garden. "Didn't I see you in the garden with Jesus?" he asked (v. 26, P). Once more Peter denied his association with Jesus, and instantly he heard a cock crowing.

Peter's mind must have flashed back at once to the conversation at supper. "I will lay down my life for you," he had said to Jesus. "Will you lay down your life for me?" Jesus had asked. "Truly, truly, I say to you, the cock will not crow, till you have denied me three times" (13:37–38).

Sometime between his burst of bravado in the garden and the crowing of the cock—as early as 3 a.m. in Jerusalem—Peter had lost his courage. With Jesus by his side, nothing could daunt him, not even a cohort of legionnaires. But alone in a courtyard, with a fire casting shadows on strange faces, it was a different matter. Something went out of him, and he was afraid.

I know the feeling, Lord; it happens to me. When I have been faithful at prayer, and feel your presence, I am ready for anything. My pulse races to do your will. But when I have been unfaithful and feel as if I'm on my own, it is another story. Help me today to be faithful, that no shadows may frighten me. For your name's sake. Amen.

Week 9: Saturday

John 18:28–32   A Fateful Meeting

"I believe in God the Father Almighty, maker of heaven and earth, and in Jesus Christ his only Son, our Lord, who was conceived by the Holy Ghost, born of the Virgin Mary, suffered under Pontius Pilate. . . ." Thus begins the Apostle's Creed, the most widely used affirmation of faith in Christendom. The entire creed names only two human beings beside Christ. One is his mother Mary. The other is Pontius Pilate, the Roman governor of Judea whom we meet in this section of John's Gospel.

Pilate was procurator or governor of Judea from A.D. 26–36. His reputation among Jewish authors of the period is a sordid one. Philo associated his name with robbery and murder, and Josephus accused him of horrible atrocities against the Jews. While it was his order that eventually resulted in Jesus' crucifixion, the Christian writers of the period were, curiously, less condemning. They pilloried the Jewish authorities as the real villains in the drama, and left the impression that Pilate was a more or less helpless pawn in the judicial process of the day.

The procurator's primary base was in Antioch, not Jerusalem. But Pilate had doubtless come up to the garrison headquarters in Jerusalem for the Passover feast, to be on hand to quell any disturbance that might arise during the festival. What a fateful move that was for Pilate! Who would remember his name today if he had not gotten involved with Jesus?

We do not know precisely how much power the Romans allowed the Jewish Sanhedrin in settling its own affairs. Some scholars think they were not permitted to impose the death penalty (as verse 31 attests), and so brought Jesus before Pilate on a charge of sedition against the government. Others refer to the accounts of stoning in the Gospel (8:3–5; 8:59; 10:31) and the Book of Acts (particularly the stoning of Stephen in 7:58–60) to argue that the Jews could execute by stoning, but in Jesus' case desired death by crucifixion, which carried a curse from God (Deut. 21:23) and would discredit Jesus in the eyes of his followers. Verse 32, "This was to fulfill the word which Jesus had spoken to show by what death he was to die," seems to support the latter contention. (John's reference, of course, is to 3:14, which said the Son of man must be "lifted up.")

"The Jews"—members of the Sanhedrin and their police—took Jesus to Pilate very early in the morning. The Greek indicates it was in the last division of the night, from 3:00 A.M. to 6:00 A.M. It was not uncustomary for Roman officials to be at work this early, finishing their agendas well before noon.

Ever punctilious in their religious observances, "the Jews" took Jesus only as far as the outside of the praetorium, or Roman hall, where Pilate was. Numbers 9:6 indicates that "unclean" Jews could not take the Passover meal when it was regularly celebrated, but must delay a month to allow for cleansing. Either these officials and police thought they would be contaminated by entering a house where there was leaven present (they were forbidden to come into contact with leaven at the time of the feast of unleavened bread) or they believed that entering a Gentile house would make them impure.

This was always the picture of observant Jews in the Gospels— they ridiculously tithed their little herb gardens of mint and cumin while failing to observe the weightier matters of the Law, namely, loving God and their neighbors. Raymond Brown has put it even more pointedly about these particular Jews: "They fear that ritual impurity will prevent their eating the Passover lamb, but unwittingly they are delivering up to death him who is the Lamb of God."

Pilate, perhaps impatient with the scruples shown by the Jewish mob, went outside to meet them, and asked what official judgment they had brought against Jesus. The implication is that he was not surprised by their coming. This would be explained by the presence of the soldiers in the garden a few hours earlier—he had already collaborated with the local officials by lending them a cohort of men to overpower Jesus and the disciples.

The answer given by "the Jews" hardly disguises their disdain for the Roman ruler: "If this man were not an evildoer, we would not have handed him over" (v. 30). The word for "handed over" is the same one used frequently in John to describe Judas' betrayal of Jesus. "The Jews" too were betraying him as their countryman by giving him over to the Romans.

Pilate, dissatisfied with the answer, ordered "the Jews" to take Jesus back and judge him by their own laws. It was Roman policy to leave jurisdiction as much as possible within the hands of local authorities. But they could not impose the death penalty they really desired, probably by crucifixion—implying that Jesus was a dangerous subversive and that Pilate himself should examine the case.

O God, I am often unaware of the most fateful meetings in my own life, as Pilate was. I never know when some casual conversation or minor relationship will become the turning point of my entire existence. Guide me into real awareness, that I may not miss the important connections you prepare for me, but may be ever ready to meet them with wisdom and joy. Through Jesus Christ my Lord. Amen.

WEEK 10

Week 10: Sunday

John 18:33–38a   What Is Truth?

The main theological question of Jesus' trial was the nature of his kingship. "The Jews" had apparently told Pilate that Jesus designated himself "King of the Jews." This was probably an insurrectionist title, calculated to brand Jesus as a popular revolutionary who wished to overthrow the Romans and reestablish Jewish rule over Israel.

"Are you the King of the Jews?" asked Pilate.

"Are they your words," replied Jesus, "or did someone else supply them?" (v. 34, P)

Pilate's response (v. 35) indicates a certain helplessness. After all, he was not a Jew. How could he understand the thinking and customs of the Jews? "Your own people have handed you over," he said. "What have you done?" (v. 35, P)

"My kingship is not of this world," said Jesus; "if it were, my subjects would have fought to prevent my falling into the hands of the authorities" (v. 36, P). The word for "subjects" (RSV "servants") is *hypērētes*, the same word John used for the temple police, who were the subjects of the Sanhedrin. In other words, Jesus had his own forces, as the Sanhedrin did. But he did not use them for conflict in a worldly manner, as his kingdom was not an earthly kingdom. There was possibly an indictment of "the Jews" in these words—their subjects *had* been employed in a worldly manner.

Jesus had spoken of his kingship, so Pilate legitimately concluded he was a king, or thought he was, albeit not King of the Jews.

"*You* say I am a king," said Jesus. "But I didn't come into the world for that. I came in order to witness to the truth, and my subjects are those who are of the truth" (v. 37, P). In 9:39, Jesus said he came into the world for judgment. Judgment and truth are not uncomplementary terms. Truth, in the biblical sense, is always the basis for judgment, and carries judgment with it.

Pilate's musing question "What is truth?" was a pathetic one. Facing this compelling man whom the authorities wished to execute, he probably wondered where the truth really lay. As procurator, he had a special responsibility to render truthful judgments. In the legal sense, at least, he did come to a right judgment. But he was about to go down in the annals of infamy for lacking the moral courage to *do* the truth he recognized.

> *How often, Lord, have I stood in Pilate's shoes, wondering what to do! And how many times I have erred as he did—guessing the truth but failing to do it! Let me wait before you until wisdom becomes courage and I learn to act out the truth, not merely discern what it is. For you are the way, the truth, and the life. Amen.*

Week 10: Monday

John 18:38b–40   Jesus or Barabbas

Innocent: this was Pilate's verdict. A world traveler, a hardened soldier, a seasoned administrator, he was a wary man. How many times had he faced men before—corrupt officials, offending soldiers, habitual criminals? He had seen enough to know men, and he knew Jesus was not the kind of criminal he was accused of being.

So Pilate announced to the waiting authorities and police outside the praetorium that he found no guilt in Jesus.

But—Pilate was not through. The Jews had a custom that the procurator should release one prisoner to them at Passover. Did they wish him to release Jesus?

There is no evidence outside the Gospels of the existence of such a custom, but all the Gospels refer to it. Matthew 27:15 calls it a custom of the *governor*. Mark 15:6 and Luke 23:17 say it was *Pilate's* custom. Only John speaks of it as a custom of the Jews. Perhaps Pilate had made it an annual custom as a gesture of good will to the captive nation, and thus referred to it as *their* custom.

"The Jews" shouted down the idea of releasing Jesus. "Not this man," they cried, "but Barabbas!" (v. 40).

Barabbas is not really a name but a patronym, a kind of surname referring to the father of the man. The prefix *bar* means "son," as in the name Simon *Barjonah*, or Simon the son of Jonah. So Barabbas meant "son of Abbas." The Aramaic word *abba* meant "father," so the name may have betokened "son of the father." This would have been ironic, for "the Jews" would have been asking for "son of the father's" release while seeking the death of the real Son of the Father! Some ancient manuscripts even gave Barabbas the first name of Jesus, which would have underlined the parallelism even more.

John calls Barabbas a *lēstēs*—a robber or bandit. Jewish literature of the time frequently used this word to describe insurrectionist guerrillas who roamed the countryside making daring raids and sometimes killing people as they plundered. Mark and Luke both identify Barabbas as a murderer, and Matthew says he was "a notorious prisoner" (27:16). John shows surprisingly little interest in Barabbas; for him the drama is clearly centered on Jesus and Pilate.

Could Pilate conceivably have believed that "the Jews" would ask for the release of Jesus, when they had brought Jesus to him with the express purpose of having him condemned and executed? One biblical scholar, A. Bajsić, has advanced the thesis that Pilate tried to release Jesus in order to avoid giving up Barabbas, who was apparently a popular figure in Jerusalem. As we shall see in the next few days' readings, however, Pilate was apparently convinced of Jesus' innocence. And, more than that, he seems to have taken an unusual interest in the most extraordinary prisoner he ever faced. "The Jews" may have charged Jesus with posing as a king; but Pilate, who knew about kings, recognized something royal in the man's demeanor.

Lord, Pilate said he found no crime in Jesus, yet did not use his authority to set Jesus free. Why do so many of us lack the courage to do what we know is right? Help me to live today so that what I believe is enacted in my deeds, that you may be glorified and I may rejoice in my own integrity. Amen.

Week 10: Tuesday

John 19:1–5   Behold the Man!

Scourging was the worst form of Roman beating. There were three classes of beatings—ordinary beatings, floggings, and scourgings. The third was the most barbarous. Inflicted with a leather whip into which were imbedded bits of stone and metal, it was reserved for capital offenses. It was torture, in other words, attached to execution.

The cruelty of the soldiers was not uncommon. Stationed in a foreign country where they were disliked by the populace, and subjected to strong discipline by superior officers, they often released their pent-up hostilities on unfortunate prisoners. In Jesus' case, they had a subject of abuse whose charge was that he had tried to become a king. They could therefore vent their anger on him as if he were a fallen superior.

Draping a purple robe around him and fashioning a crown of thorns for his head, they pretended he was royalty and mocked him with cries of "Hail, King of the Jews!"—as if he were a caesar and they were greeting him, "Hail, Caesar!" Circling about him in revelry, they struck him in the face—something they probably longed to do with real superiors but never dared to try.

After the beating and mockery, which he had surely observed, Pilate emerged again before the praetorium and told "the Jews," "I am bringing him out to you, that you may know that I find no crime in him" (v. 4). This is a doubly curious statement. Pilate had already announced Jesus' innocence of the charge (18:38). The scourging, moreover, was normally the prelude to execution. Had Pilate decided to have Jesus crucified, then changed his mind during the scourging? Perhaps Jesus' behavior during the beating and mocking convinced him that he could not go through with the execution.

"Here is the man!" said Pilate as the beaten figure in purple robe and crown of thorns was pushed out in their midst. *Ecce homo,* as the Latin phrase translated it—"Behold the man!"

What did Pilate mean by these words? Did he say them proudly, defiantly, as in "See what a man you are dealing with!" Or did he say it with pathos in his voice, as if to imply, "Look, he is only a broken man; why do you wish to crucify him?"

Whatever Pilate's intention in the utterance, there can be little doubt as to John's thought in including it in the passion narrative. Throughout the Gospel he has been at pains to demonstrate the humanity of the eternal Word. Jesus has thirsted, wept, loved, and now suffered. "Behold the *man.*" Not an angel or a spirit, but a man. John is not losing the chance to remind us that God has been in our midst in human flesh, loving us person to person!

O Christ, I am ashamed of the pain and indignities you suffered—you, of all people. But I realize you still suffer whenever any of your little ones are subjected to pain or indignities. Make me more aware of where this is happening today, Lord, and give me a chance to help you there. For you are the King of my life. Amen.

Week 10: Wednesday

John 19:6–11　The Limited Power of Pilate

Again the Jewish authorities refused to accept the release of Jesus. Pilate, it is clear, really desired to set Jesus free. He must have recognized in him a depth of being far beyond that of men he was accustomed to sentence. But the Jews were persistent. They had wanted Jesus' death for a long time, and were not about to let it slip through their hands now.

"Crucify! Crucify!" they shouted.

Pilate was angry. "Crucify him yourselves," he said. "I have found him innocent" (v. 6, P).

They could not do it, of course. They had brought Jesus to Pilate in the first place because only the Romans had the power of crucifixion. So they raised another issue for Pilate to consider. They had been accusing Jesus of being a political revolutionary, thinking that was a charge Pilate could not ignore. Now they shifted ground and accused him of the real basis of their animosity all along, that he had made himself the Son of God. The Jews had a law about that, they said, that carried death with it. They were probably referring to Leviticus 24:16, "He who blasphemes the name of the Lord shall be put to death." (They did not remind

Pilate, cagily, that the kind of death prescribed was death by stoning.)

This change of direction on the part of "the Jews" was tantamount to saying, "Look, we made a mistake in trying to get what we wanted by pretending that Jesus is a political insurgent. He may be innocent of that. But he is not innocent of blasphemy, and our law requires that he die. We are counting on you to help us see that he does."

Pilate, upon hearing this, was "the more afraid" (v. 8). There have been no previous references to fear on Pilate's side. What does this suggest? Perhaps Pilate was worried now for Jesus' sake. The matter of Jesus' release was becoming more complicated.

Once again Pilate took Jesus into the praetorium to question him. "Where are you from?" he asked (v. 9). Luke reports that Pilate asked Jesus if he was a Galilean and used the fact that he was as a reason to send him to Herod for judgment, as Herod was tetrarch of Galilee (23:6). John may have used the same words to indicate a totally different question. We have been reminded again and again that Jesus was from the Father, to whom he would return following the resurrection. Pilate's question is a rhetorical reminder of Jesus' true origin, not a mere question of geographical location.

Why did Jesus remain silent and not reply to the question? In the Synoptics, he remained silent through most of his interrogation, fulfilling an image of the Suffering Servant in Isaiah 53:7 who was mute like a sheep before its shearers. Here, the silence may be for one of two reasons: (1) to emphasize Jesus' regal control of the exchange with Pilate, or (2) because Jesus thought it futile to reply. He had not convinced the Jews of his heavenly origin. How could he expect the Roman prefect to understand?

Pilate chided him for his silence. "Don't you realize," he asked, "that I have the power to set you free or to crucify you?" (v. 10, P).

"No," said Jesus, in effect, "you don't. Yours is a limited power, a proscribed power. Only God, the one sending me, has power over me. The only power you have is the power he lets you have. Whatever happens, therefore, is not really your fault; it is 'the Jews'' fault. I let them take me in the garden because it was my time to do so. They are really the ones who are challenging the power of God."

Lord, I sympathize with Pilate. He was dealing with matters he could not comprehend. Much of my life seems to be lived the same way, dealing with things beyond my understanding or control. Be merciful to me, a sinner, and let me live with love and courage. For your name's sake. Amen.

Week 10: Thursday

John 19:12–16   The End of the Trial

Pilate had considered the charge that Jesus was a political enemy and had dismissed it. He had investigated the possibility that Jesus was a religious criminal and decided he was not. Once more, he went outside to "the Jews" and attempted to persuade them to let him release Jesus.

But "the Jews" were crafty. If they could not achieve Jesus' crucifixion by defaming him, they would do it by personal threats to Pilate. Jesus had admitted he was a king, and any one who set himself up as a king—even a spiritual one—was challenging Caesar, who claimed to be both a temporal and spiritual ruler. "If you release this man," said "the Jews," "you are not Caesar's friend" (v. 12).

Pilate must have blanched at this. "The Jews" were threatening to accuse him officially before Caesar. He would be subject to investigation. There was no telling what errors or corruption in his prefecture would come to light. At the very least, a cloud of suspicion would be thrown over his name. Future appointments would be jeopardized. Even his present authority might be terminated or impaired.

Some scholars believe there was a special order in the Roman Empire known as the Friends of Caesar—that it was held by those who had done special favors for Caesar or were politically well related to him. If this was so, Pilate was being taunted as well as threatened. He was not, "the Jews" were pointing out, behaving as a true Friend of Caesar. He was permitting his special regard for this Nazarene prisoner to make him forget his ordinarily unswerving allegiance to the Emperor. And any sign of softness in his administration would be ill taken by Rome!

This was the argument that crumbled Pilate. He would withstand his clever adversaries no more. Peter had denied his Lord

[133

three times. Pilate had tried three times to save him. Now Pilate could—or would—do no more.

Jesus was brought outside onto the *lithostrotos*, the place of wide paving stones. Such stones were always an evidence of an official building or a palace, for individuals could not afford them in common residences. The Hebrew word *gabbatha* is not an obvious translation of the word for pavement. Instead, it seems to mean "high" or "elevated." Possibly the porch of wide stones was elevated from the street level.

(There is an old fortress in Jerusalem, called Antonia, where excavations have revealed such a place of wide paving stones; many archaeologists favor it as the site of Pilate's confrontations with "the Jews.")

Pilate seated himself on the judgment bench, from which official sentences were decreed. John is careful to note the hour—it was twelve noon. The trial lasted six hours, including the time of the scourging and mocking of Jesus. Mark 15:25 sets the time of crucifixion at 9 a.m. But John is interested in the symbolism of a noontime crucifixion on the day before Passover—it was the very hour when the priests in the temple began to slay the thousands of lambs required for the Passover meal.

In ancient times, the lambs had been killed on the evening of the day before Passover. The law in Exodus 12:6 required that they be kept alive till then. But in more recent years, the swelling of the population in Jerusalem by tens of thousands of visitors made it impossible for the priests to get all the lambs slain between sundown and darkness. So liberal interpretation had decreed that evening might begin with the beginning of the sun's decline at noon, and that was when the priests commenced the enormous task of slaughtering thousands of animals.

"Here is your King!" said Pilate at the hour of the slaughtering. Is there an echo of John the Baptist's voice in 1:29, "Behold, the Lamb of God"? Both statements begin with the Greek *ide*, "behold" or "here is."

But "the Jews" were not having the Lamb for their King. "Away with him, crucify him!" they shouted. "Shall I crucify your King?" asked Pilate—clearly indicating that the crucifixion had to be done by Roman order. "We have no king but Caesar," replied "the Jews."

It was a damning admission—one the Jews had always been loath to make. God was the King of Israel, according to 1 Samuel 8:7, and God had only allowed Israel an earthly king as an accommodation to her blindness and wickedness. Now the authorities of Israel were owning a completely foreign king—and one who claimed to be a divinity!

The drama of the trial was over. Jesus, garbed in purple and a crown of thorns, was delivered to his crucifiers. "The Jews" had judged themselves by rejecting the eternal Word.

O Lamb of God, who takest away the sins of the world, be my King, now and forever. Amen.

Week 10: Friday

John 19:17–22 Pilate Has the Last Word

All the Gospels are remarkably taciturn about the execution of Jesus. They expand in varying degrees upon the events leading up to the crucifixion, and upon the sayings and events which follow it. But they provide little detail about the actual placing of Jesus on the cross. Either they could not bear to describe it or they revered it too much to expatiate on it.

Jesus bore his own cross, says John. This would probably have been only the crossbar; the upright beam was normally left standing at the place of execution. The Synoptics all report that Simon of Cyrene was compelled to help Jesus carry his cross. Possibly Jesus began carrying the cross alone and Simon was encountered on the way to Golgotha, which was outside the city walls. To John, it may have been theologically important to picture Jesus bearing the cross alone—he was the regal Son of God.

The place of crucifixion was known as "the place of a skull." *Golgotha* was the Hebrew word for "skull," and *calvaria* the Latin word. Tradition assumes that the crucifixion occurred on a skull-shaped hill, though the place may have been so designated because of a skull left there to mark it as a forbidden site. Ancient Christian legends attest that Adam was buried on the site, and Jesus, the bringer of eternal life, shed his blood on the skull of the first man.

"Two others" were crucified with Jesus. Mark and Matthew identify them as *lēstai* (the word used for Barabbas) or robbers, and Luke says they were criminals. Pilate may have ordered that Jesus be given the middle cross as a place of honor. The Gospels' care in observing that one man was killed on either side of Jesus may also have related to the request of James and John that they be permitted to sit on either side of him in the kingdom (Matt. 20:20–28; Mark 10:35–45; Luke 22:24–27). Jesus replied to their request by asking if they could drink the cup that he must drink, referring to the suffering of the cross.

The dominant motif of this particular Johannine passage is the information that it was Pilate who caused an inscription to be put on the cross (Matthew 27:37 says it was over Jesus' head) naming Jesus as King of the Jews. The inscription was in three primary languages, so that anyone who could read at all would comprehend the words. Apparently it was the plaque bearing a criminal's accusation, commonly carried ahead of the man or hung by a cord about his neck.

All the Gospels refer to the inscription, but only John attributes it to Pilate. His information forms a fitting climax to the drama of Pilate's struggle for the release of Jesus. Failing to persuade "the Jews" to accept the release, he printed the words of accusation on a public placard. "The Jews" objected that what he printed was inaccurate—Jesus only *said* he was King of the Jews. "What I have written I have written," said Pilate (v. 22).

It was almost a confession of faith on Pilate's part. Perhaps he did not fully understand the significance of the title—he was a foreigner and probably not a religious man. But there was something about Jesus that compelled his respect and wonder. For him, Jesus *was* the King of the Jews, even though his throne was a cross.

O Lord, how did Pilate live with what he saw that day? I am grieved merely to read about it. Grant that I may never stray very far from this tragic scene, except to experience the joy of your resurrection. For you are the Risen One with nailprints in your hands. Amen.

Week 10: Saturday

John 19:23–25a   The Tunic of Jesus

John alone has told us that the soldiers who crucified Jesus were a quaternion—a band of four. It is possible that a quaternion was assigned to each man being crucified.

When the soldiers had put Jesus on the cross, they exercised their privilege of dividing his belongings among themselves. Scholars have written entire books speculating on what the four garments were. There is agreement that three would have been a *tallith,* or robe; a cincture or girdle; and a head covering of some kind, probably like a modern *kafia.* The fourth article was probably Jesus' sandals, unless he was wearing an undershirt beneath his tunic.

The tunic was a garment usually worn next to the skin. The seamlessness of Jesus' tunic did not indicate that it was particularly expensive or valuable. It was merely in keeping with a law in Leviticus 19:19 that forbade wearing a garment woven of two kinds of material. Tunics and robes that had not been pieced together were common in the marketplace, for this showed at a glance that the law was honored.

The soldiers cast lots for the tunic to avoid cutting it up for division. John saw this as fulfilling a prophecy in Psalm 22:18 about a man's enemies dividing his possessions among them. Psalm 22, incidentally, is the one beginning "My God, my God, why hast thou forsaken me?," cited by Mark 15:34 as one of Jesus' words from the cross. John would not have quoted this verse of the psalm because of his emphasis on the constant unity of the Son with the Father. (Several early church fathers, it should be noted, saw in the seamless tunic a symbol of the unity theme so prominent throughout the Gospel.)

One can hardly resist speculating about the soldier who won the toss and received Jesus' tunic. Did he wear it as his own undergarment, against the skin? Did he feel the aura of its last owner, and did it lead to any dramatic effects in his life?

Jesus was apparently left naked on the cross, as most men wore either a tunic or a breechcloth beneath their clothing, but not both. He died therefore as he had come into the world—without property or clothing.

O Lord, you were the victim of such humiliation, yet turned it into glory and triumph. Help me to love you so much that I will not worry about my own defeats in the world, but will rejoice in the light of your victory. For yours is the kingdom forever. Amen.

WEEK 11

Week 11: Sunday

John 19:25b–27   The True Holy Family

The previous scene (verses 23–25*a*) revealed four soldiers. This one has four women—Jesus' mother, his aunt, and the two other Marys. According to one scholar who has studied the matter thoroughly, the families of those crucified were usually permitted to remain by the side of their dying relatives. We know from the Synoptics that Jesus traveled in the company of a number of women, as well as his disciples, and that his mother was often in the group.

Looking down from the cross, Jesus saw his mother among the women standing there. At a slight distance stood also the beloved disciple John. "Woman," Jesus said—the word he had used to address her at the wedding in Cana (2:4)—"behold, your son!" To John, he said: "Behold, your mother!"

It was a transaction similar to ancient contract scenes in which a dying man made provision for a wife or children or parents being left behind. Perhaps Jesus, who had known what kind of death he must die, had made the arrangements earlier, and now, in the final hour of his consciousness, was sealing what had been decided.

The Gospel of John has no birth narrative for Jesus, and so contributes nothing to the story of the holy family as found in

138]

Matthew and Luke. But it has this touching scenario in which Mary, the mother of Jesus, is given into the care of the disciple John. In other words, it gives us the picture of another kind of holy family—one built on the mutual love and commitment of the members.

In this sense, the picture prefigures the nature of all Christian fellowship. Those of us who are one with Jesus and God are also one with each other. Jesus has commanded us to love one another (15:17). We are to care not only for Jesus but for all those who are of his family.

What a tender picture, O God, of the life in your Son. How different it is from the world, where we dwell in isolation and loneliness. Grant that I may truly care for others in the fellowship, and share whatever I have with them, for your Son's sake. Amen.

Week 11: Monday

John 19:28–30 It Is Finished

We have dwelled at length upon these brief passages of the Gospel because they are so filled with meaning and importance. Here, in a mere forty-five words (in the Greek), John describes the final minutes of Jesus' dying, including two of the seven sayings on the cross.

Knowing the work he had been sent to do was completed, Jesus said, "I thirst."

Three observations may be offered:

(1) This fulfilled a prophecy, as John points out. The probable allusion is to Psalm 69:21, "For my thirst they gave me vinegar to drink."

(2) To this point, Jesus had held himself in rigorous self-control. He retained regal composure throughout the trial and crucifixion. With his work finished, he now indulged a personal need and asked for a drink.

(3) With this detail, absent from the other Gospels, John was once more enforcing his theme of the humanity of Jesus. The messiah who had described himself to the Samaritan woman as the

giver of "living water" (4:10) was also a man of flesh and blood, with appetites like those of ordinary persons. This was no docetic Christ. He was a human being in the fullest sense of the words.

A jar or bowl of vinegar stood near the cross. The word for vinegar, *oxos*, means a diluted, vinegary wine drunk by common people and soldiers. The jar may have been placed there by custom for the dying men, or it may simply have belonged to the soldiers or someone else. The fact that the wine was not merely held to Jesus' mouth, but was poured on a sponge and extended to him on a stick, is the clearest indication we have that the cross was a high one.

The word *hyssop* has caused commentators some concern. The hyssop bush was not uncommon, but its stalk was not notably strong, and seems an unlikely kind of stick to have used for the task of extending a sponge soaked in wine. Some scholars therefore think there may have been a scribal error in copying the word and that it was originally *hyssos*, a javelin or spear. But it is probable that John intended the word *hyssop*, because the hyssop plant was used at the time of the exodus to sprinkle the blood of the paschal lamb on the doorposts of Israelite families (Exod. 12:22). Jesus was the Lamb of God, taking away the sins of the world (1:29). It would have been extraordinarily fitting for a hyssop plant to have come in contact with his suffering body in the final moments of the crucifixion.

Having received the vinegary wine, fulfilling the scripture, Jesus said, "It is finished," bowed his head, and gave up his spirit. His work was done. If John had been present at the cross during Jesus' most agonizing moments, when he said "My God, my God, why hast thou forsaken me?" (Matt. 27:46; Mark 15:34), or if he knew the tradition of the saying, he omitted it from his narrative. Similarly, he did not mention Jesus' crying with a loud voice, "Father, into thy hands I commit my spirit!" (Luke 23:46) His Jesus simply bowed his head in a quiet manner and gave up the spirit.

John had emphasized all along the unity of the Son and the Father. This was the hour of the Son's glory. He did not vent his agony, or in any way voice misgivings about what was transpiring. For this cause he had come into the world.

Lamb of mercy, I wait reverently before this image of your crucifixion and listen as you say, "I thirst." Would, Lord, I could give you everything for which you thirst: an end to human suffering, a universal community of love, the joy of your whole creation. At least let me give you no cheap wine, but the very best I have. For your love's sake. Amen.

Week 11: Tuesday

John 19:31–37 The Wounded Side

The Jews did not like to have bodies left on crosses overnight because of a law in Deuteronomy 21:22–23 saying that the land would be defiled by a corpse remaining on a tree all night. They especially did not want the bodies of Jesus and the other men crucified with him left on their crosses, because Passover that year coincided with the sabbath, making it a particularly holy occasion. So they went to Pilate and asked that the legs of the crucified men be broken to hasten their dying.

The Romans were usually in no hurry to remove the bodies. Sometimes people died slowly, over a period of days. Besides, corpses left on crosses were a deterrent to crime. But apparently Pilate wanted no trouble from these bothersome people who had threatened to report him to Rome (19:12), so he sent the delegation they requested.

Breaking an executed man's legs was not an unusual practice. Called the *crurifragium*, it was accomplished with a large mallet. The skeleton of a first-century man discovered in recent excavations in Jerusalem had both legs broken, leading archaeologists to suspect that he had died as a criminal.

Jesus' legs were not broken, because the soldiers saw that he was already dead. True to John's portrait of him, he remained in control of his own death, dying before the soldiers came.

One of the soldiers, however, apparently to be sure Jesus was dead, plunged a spear into his side. At once, says John, "there came out blood and water" (v. 34).

Much has been written of the blood and water, by both medical doctors and biblical scholars. The doctors have been at pains to show how blood and water could possibly have flowed from the side of a dead man, as blood does not generally flow after the heart stops beating, and the water is even more difficult to explain. The biblical scholars have taxed their minds to cite theological reasons for the unusual event. One of the simplest of these is found in the Gospel itself, when Jesus stood at the Feast of Tabernacles and spoke of "rivers of living waters" flowing from the faithful person (7:38).

The early church fathers may have had the best attitude. They regarded the event as a miracle, and saw verse 35, about the witness (surely John himself), as proof of this. An ordinary event, they reasoned, would not have required the special testimony of a witness.

Whether it was a natural occurrence or a miraculous happening, John doubtless had a symbological reason for including it in his narrative. The water is rich in associations—the water from the rock struck by Moses in the wilderness (Num. 20:10–11)—the water of life—the water of baptism. The coming of the Spirit was also associated with water, as John 3:5 attests: "Truly, truly, I say to you, unless one is born of water and the Spirit, he cannot enter the kingdom of God." And the imagery of blood is just as strong as that of water in Hebrew lore—the blood of the Passover lambs—the blood of covenants—the blood containing the spirit of life.

Considering the great sacramental passages of John—references to baptism and new birth in 3:3–7 and to the Eucharist in 6:1–14, 25–59—there is a likelihood that the author intended this reference to blood and water to be sacramental also. Jesus had finished the work the Father gave him by dying on the cross. Thus both baptism and the Lord's Supper would ever after derive their real meaning from the drama of Calvary—a drama that in its climax contained references to both of them.

The soldiers had not broken Jesus' legs, and they had pierced his side. The scriptures, said John, foretold both. Exodus 12:46 says, of the Passover lamb, "you shall not break a bone of it." And Zechariah 12:10 says, "I will pour out on the house of David and the inhabitants of Jerusalem a spirit of compassion and supplication, so that, when they look on him whom they have pierced, they shall mourn for him, as one mourns for an only child, and weep bitterly over him, as one weeps over a first-born."

The passion story would indeed invoke the tears of those who belonged to the true Jerusalem, the new Israel. Not because Jesus had died—the resurrection would cancel all grief for that—but because he had suffered so for the sins of others.

"They shall look on him whom they have pierced." What had John said in 3:14—that as the serpent was lifted up in the wilderness and the people were saved by looking at it, so Jesus must be lifted on the cross? Now it would happen. People would look and be saved.

O Jesus, born to die but alive forevermore, help me to turn my eyes upon you. "Let the water and the blood, from thy wounded side that flowed, be of sin the double cure, save from wrath and make me pure." Amen.

Week 11: Wednesday

John 19:38–42   The Secret Disciples

How encouraging this passage must have been to Jewish Christians afraid to confess Jesus in the synagogues! At last, two members of the Sanhedrin, the council that had sought Jesus' death, came forward to claim his body and display their allegiance to him. Mark 15:43 and Luke 23:50 both identify Joseph as a member of the council, and we know from John's report of the meeting between Nicodemus and Jesus (3:1–14) that Nicodemus was too.

Jesus had said in 12:32, speaking of his death on the cross, "When I am lifted up from the earth, I will draw all men to myself." Was this part of what he meant—that even the secret followers among the rulers of Israel would come out of hiding to own their discipleship?

Matthew 27:60 says the place of burial was in Joseph's "own new tomb." As Mary had used her burial ointment to anoint Jesus (John 12:1–8), Joseph was surrendering his own resting place. The body was washed, covered in the mixture of myrrh and aloes, and wrapped in linen cloths. The amount of myrrh and aloes was very great—enough, in fact, to indicate that Nicodemus regarded Jesus as a person of royal status. The fact that the tomb was in a garden also betokens the royal nature of the burial—kings and rulers were usually buried in such surroundings, while common people were buried in ordinary burial grounds. It was only fitting, after the emphasis on Jesus' kingship throughout the trial and crucifixion, that he be interred in a royal manner.

To comprehend the daring of Joseph and Nicodemus in

preparing the body and burying it, we need to remember the Jewish associations of death and defilement. "He who touches the dead body of any person," says Numbers 19:11, "shall be unclean seven days." This meant that the two men could not eat the Passover meal the evening of Christ's death. Their families and friends would know they had been defiled. There was no way of keeping their devotion secret any longer.

We can only suppose they had discovered something that made their risk worthwhile—that the one who died on the cross was the real Passover Lamb, who takes away the sins of the world!

Lord, I have seen the pilgrims in Jerusalem kneeling to kiss the stone where your body was prepared for burial. I wanted to join them, but decided it was probably not the very stone on which you were laid. Give me a simple faith, I pray, that I may feel at all times the mystery of your presence and serve you as the King of my life. For your kingdom's sake. Amen.

Week 11: Thursday

John 20:1–10   The Empty Tomb

This passage is so vibrant with meaning and mystery that it is difficult for a Christian to read it without trembling. For two chapters, we have been reading about the capture, trial, and execution of Jesus. The material was heavy, sorrowful, dirgelike. Now the pace quickens and the material lightens. Suddenly people are running and speaking breathlessly to one another. There is excitement, hope, the dawning of belief. The entire atmosphere is different.

It was early Sunday morning, the day after Passover sabbath. Mary of Magdala, a small town in Galilee only a few miles from Capernaum, came to the tomb where Jesus was laid on Friday evening. She had stood with Jesus' mother near the cross less than forty-eight hours earlier (19:25). Now she was coming to mourn his death—to weep and wail in the Israelite fashion. (In 11:31, the Jews who saw another Mary rise and go out to meet Jesus assumed she was going to weep at Lazarus' tomb.) Some interpreters assume she was not alone, because of the plural pronoun when she said "we do not know where they have laid him" (v. 2). Perhaps the mother of Jesus and the other women were with her or followed at a short distance.

At any rate, Mary found the stone rolled away from the mouth of the tomb and ran to inform the disciples. "They have taken the Lord out of the tomb," she said (v. 2). We cannot be sure who she meant by "they," if indeed she had a specific group of persons in mind. Perhaps she believed the soldiers or the Jewish authorities had done it. Or she may have thought grave-robbers were responsible, for there is evidence to show that corpse-stealing was a serious problem in those days.

Peter and John ("the other disciple, the one whom Jesus loved") ran toward the tomb. John, perhaps because he was younger and more excitable, arrived first. By this time, the first rays of the sun had broken over the garden. John knelt to peer through the small opening, and saw the linen cloths used to wrap Jesus' body lying there on the stone shelf that ran around three sides of the cavernous tomb.

Before John could recover from the sight, Peter had arrived and plunged through the opening into the interior of the tomb. True to his impetuous nature, he was not worried about ceremonial defilement from contact with the dead. In the shadowy half-light, he saw not only the linen cloths but the *soudarion*, or head covering, which instead of lying with the linen cloths was rolled up and lying by itself. Unable to believe his senses, Peter doubtless shouted this information to John. If robbers had stolen the body, they would not have troubled to unwrap the spiced grave clothes and lay the head covering neatly to the side. The disciples were clearly dealing with something greater than a body-theft!

John soon followed Peter inside and saw the evidence too. "Then the other disciple, who reached the tomb first, also went in, and he saw and believed" (v. 8). Many scholars have argued on the basis of these words that John came to faith in the resurrected Jesus before Peter did. It seems probable, however, that Peter's belief is implied in the narrative. The word *also* is the same in Greek as the word *and*, and the construction of verse 8 permits us to read "he also saw and believed." This interpretation is strengthened by verse 9, "for as yet they did not know the scripture, that he must rise from the dead." The plural pronoun has the force of implying that *both* Peter and John had seen and believed inside the tomb.

That the disciples did not know "the scripture" pertaining to the resurrection may strike us as very unusual, for in the Synoptic Gospels Jesus often alluded to his resurrection and New Testament writers often combed the Old Testament for possible allusions to the resurrection. But we should remember that John has consistently emphasized Jesus' reunion with the Father, not his resurrection as such. Repeatedly, in the farewell speech and prayer of chapters fourteen to seventeen, Jesus spoke of going away and being with the Father—not of shortly returning to the disciples.

It was natural, therefore, that the two disciples, on making the astounding discovery of Jesus' resurrection, returned to their homes (v. 10). (They were not, apparently, living at the same address in Jerusalem.) Their heads were filled with the wonder of what they had seen, but they did not anticipate seeing Jesus again before they too went to be with the Father. They were probably quite content with the evidence that Jesus was triumphant over death.

> *Lord, my heart beats faster and faster as I contemplate this marvelous scripture. How simply and beautifully it describes the wonder of that irrepeatable scene! I can enter the amazement of it as if I were there. Thank you for this vivid memory from the two disciples and what it has meant to believers through the ages. Let it remain strong and active in my mind throughout this day and the days to come, transforming the way I view the world and my role in it. For you have overcome everything—even my lethargy. Amen.*

Week 11: Friday

John 20:11–18   The Appearance to Mary Magdalene

This is surely one of the tenderest scenes in the entire Bible. There is little wonder it supplied the inspiration for C. Austin Miles's famous hymn "In the Garden," with its description of intimate companionship with Jesus.

Mary apparently followed Peter and John back to the tomb, arriving after they had departed for their homes (v. 10). Her "weeping" would not have been the usual mourning for the dead, as she was still concerned about the missing body. It was probably a combination of sadness, despair, and confusion.

In a distraught state of mind, she stooped, as John had, to peer into the tomb, and had a parapsychological experience. Sitting on the stone shelf where the body of Jesus had been were two angels. "Woman, why are you weeping?" they asked her. "Because they have taken away my Lord," she said, "and I do not know where they have laid him" (v. 13).

Still in the grip of the experience, Mary turned, aware of a figure behind her. In her stooping position, she did not see the figure directly, and assumed it was the keeper of the garden. (She may have seen the keeper elsewhere in the garden when she entered.) The voice behind her repeated the question of the angels: "Woman, why are you weeping? Whom do you seek?" (v. 15)

Supposing it was the gardener, Mary asked if he knew where the body was. Perhaps, as the keeper of the place, he had for some reason removed it and laid it in another tomb.

Jesus spoke her name: "Mary."

Instantly she turned and knew him.

"Rabboni!" she exclaimed.

It was the Hebrew word for teacher or master, but in a special form of the word indicating an affectionate relationship. Perhaps we can translate it "Dear Master." During Jesus' ministry, his followers probably called him rabbi more than anything else. It was instinctive of Mary to greet him as her rabbi—only she gave it this intimate form.

It has always interested readers that Mary recognized Jesus the moment he spoke her name. The passage suggests the intimate relationship that always exists between Jesus and the individual believer. And it echoes something Jesus had said in the Beautiful Shepherd passage: "The sheep hear [the shepherd's] voice, and he calls his own sheep by name" (10:3).

Apparently, as there is no evidence of Mary's having risen from her stooping position, Mary clutched at Jesus' feet when she recognized him. It would have been an appropriate gesture— prostrating oneself before an exalted master.

But Jesus said, "Don't try to hold onto me—I haven't yet ascended to the Father. Instead, go to my brothers and tell them I am ascending to my Father and your Father, my God and your God" (v. 17, P).

"Do not hold me." Jesus was probably alluding to the very nature of psychic experiences like this one. Mary was still flesh and blood. She could not remain in this ecstatic state indefinitely, any more than any of us can. What was important was that she had seen the resurrected Lord and was to witness about this to the disciples.

The nature of the resurrection appearances in John's Gospel is already becoming clear. Jesus' rejoining the Father—his Father and ours, as verse 17 emphasizes—was the thing of supreme importance to John. The appearances were only brief manifestations to Jesus' followers in evidence of his ascension, so they would not be tempted merely to think the body had been stolen or appropriated by the authorities.

Therefore there is no real contradiction in Jesus' telling Mary not to hold him (v. 17) and then instructing Thomas to handle his wounds (v. 27). Everything is told to verify the one overriding claim of the Gospel, that the Word that became flesh has overcome the world and been reunited with the Father.

Mary, like a faithful witness, went back and reported to the disciples what she had seen and heard. This time she did not use the word *Rabboni*. She said: "I have seen the Lord."

> *Like Mary, Lord, I want the reality of sacred moments to linger forever, so that it transcends all other realities. But, like Mary, I cannot hold you. The world is too much with me. Only in prayer and meditation can I experience the union with you and the Father that overcomes the world. Therefore help me to pray as constantly as possible, and to retain the sense of having prayed even when I must be doing other things. For there is nothing like being in your presence, which even the tomb could not contain. Amen.*

Week 11: Saturday

John 20:19–23 The Recommissioning of the Disciples

In the early morning, when Peter and John had discovered the mystery of the empty tomb with the grave clothes lying neatly inside, they had returned to their separate places of residence. Then, in the evening, they were with the other disciples—all except Thomas—in the same place. Probably it was in the upper room where they had eaten the Last Supper. The doors were shut, and probably locked, "for fear of the Jews" (v. 19). Possibly they were afraid, now that the sabbath was over, that the authorities would round up Jesus' associates—or that they would be blamed for the disappearance of the body!

We can imagine their excitement as they pondered what Peter and John had seen that morning and talked of Mary Magdalene's experience with the Master in the garden. Surely they were trying to recall all of Jesus' words the night before the crucifixion, when he spoke so much about being one with the Father and going to prepare a place for them.

Suddenly, as they talked, Jesus appeared in their midst. There is no mention of the doors being opened. Instead, he simply appeared to them. *"Shālōm hālēkem,"* he said—"Peace be with you." It was the formula spoken by God to Gideon in Judges 6:23 when Gideon was frightened at seeing the Lord's angel. Only now it bore the added meaning given by Jesus in his farewell speech when he said, "In me you may have peace. . . . I have overcome the world" (16:33).

After showing the disciples his hands and side—emphasizing the brokenness of the body now raised up before them—Jesus repeated the words "Peace be with you." They were to understand that God's peace keeps even one whose body is mutilated in the kingdom's service. And this time Jesus added the Johannine form of the Great Commission: "As the Father has sent me, so I send you." The Father had sent the Son into a world of resistance and cruelty, where he had had nails driven into his hands and a spear thrust into his side. Now Jesus was sending his disciples into the same world. He had already warned them that the world would hate them as it had hated him (15:18–20).

When he had said this, Jesus breathed on the disciples and said: "Receive the Holy Spirit" (v. 22). Literally, the words may be read, "Receive holy breath," for the Greek word *pneuma* may mean either "breath" or "spirit" and there is no definite article in the sentence. Whichever way the phrase is translated, the meaning is essentially the same: Jesus was imparting his essential being to the disciples, that they might continue his work in the world. They would have his power to forgive or not forgive sins in the people they encountered.

To understand this final part of the commission (v. 23), we can turn to a similar saying of Jesus in Matthew 16:19, following Peter's confession that Jesus was the Christ: "I will give you the keys of the kingdom of heaven, and whatever you bind on earth shall be bound in heaven, and whatever you loose on earth shall be loosed in heaven." The image is of a master giving a steward the keys to all his possessions, so that the steward can act in the master's behalf for members of the household or others who require anything. The gift of his Spirit was Jesus' way of conferring total stewardship on the disciples.

One of the fascinating things about this brief passage is the number of references it bears to the form of early Christian worship, so that we could almost take it as a prototype of a worship service. *First*, the meeting took place on the first day of the week, as Christian worship did. *Second*, it occurred behind closed doors (early Christians often met in hiding). *Third*, the followers of Jesus were probably talking about their earlier experiences of Jesus. *Fourth*, Jesus manifested himself to them, as Christians believed he would in the Eucharist (*Maranatha*, "Our Lord, come," was the standard eucharistic prayer). *Fifth*, Jesus said, "Peace be with you," the formula greeting used in the Eucharist from earliest times. *Sixth*, the followers received the gift of the Spirit. And, *seventh*, they were empowered to represent Jesus in their dealings with others.

Lord, the scripture says the disciples were glad when they saw you. I too am glad when I feel your presence. Come, I pray, behind the closed doors of my life, and breathe your Spirit upon me, that I may feel empowered to represent you in the world. For your peace is all the armor I need. Amen.

WEEK 12

Week 12: Sunday

John 20:24–29 The Great Confession

How did Thomas feel about being absent when Jesus appeared to the disciples? He must have been terribly disappointed—perhaps even resentful. We can imagine his saying, "What had you been drinking? I can't believe you really saw him." When the disciples protested that Jesus had even shown them his wounded hands and side, Thomas replied: "I would not believe it unless I could actually touch the nailprints and put my hand in his side" (v. 25, P).

But Thomas was not left out. One week later (the Jews counted the present day when figuring time, so that the eighth day corresponded to our seventh), Jesus appeared again to the disciples. This time Thomas was present. The similarities of the passage in verses 19–23 to a service of worship and the emphasis on the fact that both appearances were on Sunday or the Lord's Day suggests that these two occurrences were regarded by John as the original experiences of Christian worship.

Again, as before, Jesus came when the doors were shut, and said, "Peace be with you" (v. 26). Then, as he had earlier shown the disciples his wounded self, he offered himself to Thomas. "Put your finger here," he said, "and see my hands; and put out your hand, and place it in my side; do not be faithless, but believing" (v. 27).

Even more certainly than in verses 19–23, because of the repetition, we are dealing with references to the Eucharist. Jesus' hands represent his body or the bread, while the wounded side, from which flowed blood and water (19:34), represents the blood or the wine. The injunction to have faith, and not be disbelieving, would be especially relevant to persons approaching the sacred table. With faith, they would recall the Lord's presence in the elements. He would come and stand in their midst.

Thomas's response to the invitation of Jesus was precisely the one desired of every follower of Christ: "My Lord and my God!" It was the highest word of personal confession spoken in the entire Gospel. Jesus had been called Lamb of God, Teacher, Lord, and King of Israel. He had called himself the Bread of Life; the Light of the World; the Resurrection and the Life; the Gate of the Sheep; the Beautiful Shepherd; the Way, the Truth, and the Life; and the True Vine. But Thomas's confession topped them all. It was the climax of understanding toward which the whole Gospel had been moving. And it is the insight to which every follower should rise each time he or she participates in Christian worship: "My Lord and my God!"

"Have you believed becaue you have seen me?" asked Jesus. "Blessed are those who have not seen and yet believe" (v. 29). In the Eucharist, we all see by faith. We have not really seen, as Thomas did—not literally, with our eyes. But we have seen with our hearts, and that was finally how Thomas had to see too.

My Lord and my God: it is a staggering confession, and I feel the weight of it as I make it. It changes the center of my life. I am no longer there, but you are. Come, Lord Jesus, and take full possession of me. For you are the one who died and is alive, and I want no life outside of yours. Amen.

Week 12: Monday

John 20:30–31 Life in His Name

These verses are actually a formal conclusion to the first twenty chapters of the Gospel, suggesting the possibility that the Gospel originally ended here and an editor subsequently added chapter twenty-one. This does not mean that chapter twenty-one is not authentically Johannine—only that it was appended later to the first version of the Gospel. The stories in chapter twenty-one may well have been told by John and preserved by one of his disciples until they were safely included in the written narrative

"Jesus did many other signs in the presence of the disciples," the ending says. Some of these marvelous events are doubtless recorded in other Gospels. But it is thrilling to think that what was written in the Gospels was only a portion of what Jesus did and said during his ministry with the disciples. Imagine! There were probably dozens of major healings and dramatic encounters—perhaps hundreds—that did not get into the pages of the Gospels. The authors selected only the stories and sayings needed to present a true picture of Jesus' power and personality.

The "signs" included in his Gospel, says John, were put there so that the reader "may believe that Jesus is the Christ, the Son of God, and . . . have life in his name" (v. 31).

Scholars disagree about whether the verb "to believe" (*pisteuēte*) is an aorist or a present subjunctive. John's customary use of causal relationships in other places argues for the present subjunctive. In this case, the verb should be translated "keep believing" or "continue to believe." That is, "these are written in order that you may continue to believe that Jesus is the Christ, the Son of God," etc.

This would agree with our contention that the entire Gospel was written primarily to encourage Jewish Christians to continue in the faith, even if expelled from their synagogues, not to make new Christians. It would also help to explain why John presents a more exalted image of Jesus than the other Gospels—it was purposely intensified to appeal to persons who already had a basic introduction to the faith but needed a more "spiritual" narrative to deepen their perceptions of Christ and his faithfulness as the shepherd of the Christian flock.

The object of all this? That readers might have life in Jesus' name. As we said in the beginning, John's is the Gospel of eternal life—of a quality of existence that is truly extraordinary. And people discover that dimension of life through faith in the One who came among us as the Wisdom of God.

Lord, when I think how many wonderful signs have been done in your name, both during your ministry and since you breathed your Spirit into

the disciples, my mind is boggled! They continued to be done throughout the world every hour! Give me eyes to see and ears to hear, that I may always have life in your name. For you are the Christ, the Son of God. Amen.

Week 12: Tuesday

John 21:1–11 An Amazing Catch

This chapter has long perplexed scholars. It is obviously an appendage to the first twenty chapters, which ended with 20:31. The language and usages are largely Johannine, however, suggesting that the material was added by a disciple of John if not John himself. But why was it added? And why, after the Gospel was so largely centered in Jerusalem, was this episode set in Galilee by the seashore?

The answer may lie in the symbolism of the sea and the fish, and their relation to the universal mission of the church. The first twenty chapters of John were concerned with the ministry of Jesus and its immediate effect on the faith of the disciples. But Jesus, after his "hour" had come, was returning to the Father. He had breathed his Spirit into the disciples (20:22). Now they were to carry on his work in the world. Chapter twenty-one was necessary to dramatize the opportunities and responsibilities of their ministry. And, as the Sea of Galilee bordered on Gentile territory, it was a natural setting for a long, enacted parable about the work of the disciples and the early church.

Interestingly, there were only seven disciples who went fishing on the Sea of Tiberias or Galilee. This in itself is a clue to the meaning of the narrative. Seven, in Jewish numerology, was a universal number. It was believed there were seventy Gentile nations—seven (for universal) times ten (for wholeness or completeness).

Peter and his friends went fishing at night—a natural time to go, as fishermen usually brought in their catches to sell early in the morning. But we remember that night and darkness in John are symbolic of the world and its opposition to God. So, when the disciples caught nothing, we know why: they were fishing in their own power.

Jesus appeared with the daybreak. The Light of the World was standing on the beach. But, because it was the spiritual Jesus, who had been raised from the dead, the disciples did not recognize him. They were like the woman at the well (4:7–42), who did not know at first to whom she was talking.

"Children, have you any fish?" said Jesus. The Greek word used for children is *paidia*, which means "small boys" or "lads." It is the plural of the word used in 6:9 for the small boy brought to Jesus with the loaves and fishes, suggesting perhaps a link between the two "multiplication" stories.

Being told that the disciples had caught nothing, Jesus told them to drop their nets on the right side of the boat. Presumably they had been fishing from the left side. When they did as instructed, they caught such an amazing draft of fishes that they were unable to get the net into the boat.

The miraculous nature of the event is underlined by the fact that they were fishing essentially the same water they had fished moments earlier without success. They merely let down the nets on the opposite side of the boat.

It was John, the one who at the Last Supper had lain with his head at Jesus' bosom, who recognized the Master. Turning to Peter, who had been his companion at the empty tomb, he said, "It is the Lord!"

The picture of Peter—bold, impetuous, and impatient—is the one with which we have become familiar. Learning the identity of the One on the shore, he could not wait for the boat to get there, but dove into the sea and struck out for his Lord! We are reminded of Matthew 14:28–33 and the story of Peter's walking on the water to come to Jesus. The oddity of Peter's pausing to put on his clothes is probably best explained in terms of the difficulty of the Greek text, which can also mean "to tuck in" one's clothes. Peter was fishing in his cincture and tunic, both undergarments. When he realized that the Stranger was Jesus, he tucked up his tunic in his cincture and plunged into the water.

When the disciples got the boat to land, they found bread and a fire with a fish cooking on it. Jesus instructed them to bring some of the fish they had caught. Again Peter was the active one. Returning to the boat, he loosened the end of the net and dragged it ashore, teeming with fish.

There has been much speculation about whether the number 153 is symbolic, and, if so, what it was intended to mean. Jerome, one of the early interpreters, said that Greek zoologists recorded 153 varieties of fish in the seas and that therefore the number indicated the fullness of the church's evangelistic promise. Augustine said that 153 is the sum of all the numbers from 1 to 17, and that 17 is a combination of 7 (universality) and 10 (completeness). A more recent interpreter has observed that the number can be represented by three equilateral triangles with sides of 17 dots, combining the number 17 with the Trinity. John may have intended only to indicate a great number of fish; but, if we conclude that there was special significance in the number, it seems doubtless that the symbolism had to do with fullness or completeness.

An interesting detail is provided in verse 11, that "although there were so many, the net was not broken." This is in contrast to Luke's version of a miraculous catch, when there were so many fish that the nets broke (Luke 5:6). As we are obviously dealing with references to "catching men" (Luke 5:10 makes this plain), there is surely significance in John's information. Its most likely reference is to Jesus' faithfulness in keeping all those who believe, as expressed in 17:11–12, "And now I am no more in the world, but they are in the world, and I am coming to thee. Holy Father, keep them in thy name, which thou hast given me, that they may be one, even as we are one. While I was with them, I kept them in thy name, which thou hast given me; I have guarded them, and none of them is lost but the son of perdition, that the scripture might be fulfilled."

This passage, then, is clearly about the work of the early church as it set out to evangelize the world. Without Christ, the disciples would have been powerless. With him, they brought in great numbers of people. And, because of the unity of converts with the Son and the Father, true believers were never lost—"the net was not torn."

Thank you, Lord, for this graphic picture of the ministry of the early church. Help me to ponder it in considering the mission of the church today—and to take my place at the nets. For you are the Lord, and we listen to your voice. Amen.

Week 12: Wednedsay

John 21:12–14   Breakfast by the Sea

Having made his point about the missionary enterprise of the early church (vv. 2–11), John now turns to the manner in which the early church would be sustained, and shows us this beautiful picture of Jesus feeding his disciples. It is the only story we have, in any of the Gospels, of a breakfast meal.

The wording of verse 13, "Jesus came and took the bread and gave it to them, and so with the fish," is particularly suggestive of the serving of the Eucharist. That the meal consisted of bread and fish, and not bread and wine, is not a strong impediment to this interpretation, for we know from early Christian art (in the catacombs, for instance) that fish were often pictured as part of the communion meal. Perhaps John or his editor, noting that there was a story about wine without bread early in the Gospel (2:1–11), decided to balance the accounts near the end of the Gospel with a story about bread without wine.

The fact that all the disciples "knew it was the Lord" (v. 12) is further support for the eucharistic reference. In Luke 24:30–31, it was in the breaking of bread that the two disciples from Emmaus recognized the risen Lord. There was probably a general connection, in the minds of early Christians, between eating the Eucharist and discovering the presence of Christ—a connection to which we alluded in discussion 20:20–22 and 26–28.

This was the third time, says John, that Jesus revealed himself to the disciples after the resurrection (v. 14). This overlooks the revelation to Mary Magdalene (who of course was not one of the twelve), and numbers the two Lord's Day appearances to the disciples in Jerusalem. The stress on its being the third occasion may well mean that it too occurred on a Lord's Day, underlining once more the eucharistic reference of the passage.

The Gospel may have provided us, in the two Upper Room visits of Jesus, each on the first day of the week, and in this breakfast visit by the sea, with a normative picture of worship life in the early Christian community. From the first Sunday after the crucifixion—that is, Easter Day itself—the Christians did not fail to meet, break bread together, and experience the presence of Christ in their midst!

O Lord known in the breaking of bread and drinking the cup, I am grateful for these powerful reminders of your suffering, and for the promise that whenever we share them in your name, you will be there, ministering to us as before. Grant that Christians everywhere may give more reverence to this sacred occasion, and that, sensing your presence, we may return doubly faithful to our mission in the world. Amen.

Week 12: Thursday

John 21:15–19   A Touching Interrogation

We have observed many times through the Gospel that it was especially directed at converts who were tempted to fall away from their faith rather than be excluded from Jewish worship in the synagogues. Apostasy (the church's word for falling away) was a widespread problem in the early church, and the Gospel writers were often concerned to encourage people not to desert Christ. By the same token, they wished to encourage those who had apostatized to return to the fold.

No example was more powerful in this encouragement than Simon Peter's, for Peter had flagrantly denied Jesus not once but three times, and then had returned to favor and become the leader of the church in Jerusalem. In the commentary on Matthew 14:22–33, I pointed out that Peter's sinking in the water when he tried to walk to Jesus, and being subsequently caught and helped into the boat by Jesus, was in fact an allegorical portrait of Peter's defection and restoration to faith.

Here, in verses 15–19, we have one of the tenderest and best-loved pictures of Peter's restoration and recommissioning by Jesus.

Three times Peter had denied his Lord (18:17, 25–27); three times his Lord questioned him, "Simon, son of John, do you love me?" The use of Peter's old name, Simon, is interesting. Perhaps, as it was his name when he first came to Jesus and, when coupled with his father's name, was his more formal designation, Jesus was using it in a legal, contractual sense. Scholars have shown that repeating questions and vows three times was often done in ancient times to indicate the contractual status of a verbal exchange. The entire scene may therefore have constituted a formal commissioning of Peter to special responsibilities in the fledgling church.

The first time Jesus questioned Peter, he said, "Lovest thou me more than these?" We cannot be certain what "these" refers to, for there is no clear antecedent. Some interpreters think it infers "things"—that is, "Lovest thou me more than these things?" If that was the case, Jesus probably gestured toward the boat, the nets, and the sea, and Peter was having to choose between his old occupation and a new one. Others believe Jesus meant the disciples—did Peter love him more than they did? He *had* sworn, before his denials, that he would lay down his life for Jesus (13:37). This interrogation accords well with verses 18–19, which speak of Peter's future death in the service of Christ.

Each time that Peter replied to a question, "Yes, Lord, you know that I love you," Jesus directed him to care for his (Jesus') sheep. The first time, Jesus said, "Feed my lambs." The second time he said, "Tend my sheep." The word "tend" (Greek *poimainain*) is a broader word than "feed" (Greek *boskein*), and means "lead," "guard," and "provide for" as well as "feed." The distinction between feeding lambs and tending sheep may have been intended, for, as any shepherd knows, the lambs follow the flock and require less attention than the sheep themselves. But the third directive, "Feed my little sheep" (not merely "sheep," as in the RSV; the Greek word is different), returns to the verb used in the first directive, minimizing the probability of a strong distinction.

Peter's responses are touching, particularly the third time, when we are told that he was hurt by Jesus' repetition of the question "Do you love me?" and replied, in a final burst of desperation, "Lord, you know everything; you know that I love you" (v. 17). How could Peter prove it? He had already denied his Lord after promising to die for him. Now the only appeal was to Jesus' intimate knowledge of him. Surely Jesus knew what was in his heart, and understood how faithful he would be now that Jesus was alive forever more!

Jesus' replies, on the other hand, that Peter should feed and care for his little ones, were his way of accepting Peter's love and giving him responsibility at the same time. It was tantamount to saying, "Yes, I know you love me, and you shall show it through my flock which I entrust to you."

"Truly, truly," said Jesus, "I say to you, when you were young, you girded yourself and walked where you would; but when you are old, you will stretch out your hands, and another will gird you and carry you where you do not wish to go" (v. 18). This, says John, was to signify what kind of death Peter was to die.

It was natural for Jesus to connect death with the feeding of sheep, for they had been connected in his own ministry. When he identified himself as the Beautiful Shepherd, he added immediately, "The beautiful shepherd lays down his life for the sheep" (10:11). The servant, he had told the disciples, is not greater than the master (15:20).

There may have been an old proverb behind Jesus' saying. If there was, it has been lost. But the meaning is clear. When Peter was younger, he was self-determinant—he hitched up his belt, went where he wanted, and did what he wished. Now that he had the responsibility for Christ's little ones, it would not be so easy. The time would come when he would stretch forth his hands, be bound by others, and carried where he had no desire to go. This was the way it had been with Jesus; he had been bound in the garden of Gethsemane and taken to Annas and Pilate. And Peter would have a similar experience, leading to his own crucifixion.

Finally Jesus said simply, "Follow me."

Follow him where? Wherever he led. Back to Jerusalem. To Joppa. To Macedonia. To Rome. Eventually to death and complete union with the Father.

> Lord, this is a model commissioning service. Peter is tested, he answers that he loves you, you tell him to care for your sheep, and you predict his death in the ministry. Help me to love you so much that I too will be ready to die in your service. For you are the Beautiful Shepherd and you have laid down your life for me. Amen.

Week 12: Friday

John 21:20–23   What about the Other Person?

There has been much speculation about the reason for the existence of this brief passage. Was it written to correct the impression that John would live until the *parousia* or return of Jesus? Was it intended to settle a dispute among followers of Peter and followers of John as to which was greater in the kingdom? The answers are not easy.

On the surface, it is merely a little story about Peter's interest in what the beloved disciple would do while Peter was following Jesus. "Lord, what about this man?" (v. 21) Perhaps Peter wished to have John at his side. They had experienced much together as disciples—especially the discovery of the empty tomb and folded grave clothes. Or, as seems more likely, in the light of Jesus' mild rebuke, Peter wanted to know what Jesus planned for John while he himself was feeding Jesus' sheep and being led away captive.

How easy it is to understand that! We are forever trying to condition our service to Christ on what others are or are not doing for the kingdom. We give or withhold gifts on the basis of what others are giving. We go or refuse to go on the basis of whether they are going. We would do well to mark the words of Jesus addressed to Peter: "What is that to you? Follow me!" (v. 22).

Once more we need to remember the effect of the Gospel on Jewish Christians facing expulsion from their synagogues for the faith. How would they have interpreted this passage? Surely they would have heard in it the warning we have heard—to follow Christ faithfully without making the behavior of others the model for our own actions. Some Christians who read the text were actually facing death for Christ. They were not to hesitate because others were not put in the same situation. Their devotion was to Christ, not to some kind of moral consensus.

"Suppose," said Jesus in effect, "I said to John, 'You stay right here until I return for you.' Would that make any difference in what I have asked you to do? No. I have told you to follow me. You have said you love me. Now follow me!" (v. 22, P).

The rumor apparently circulated that John was not to die, but was to remain behind until Jesus returned to earth.

Those who believe the passage was written to quell competitive feelings of two groups of disciples suppose that Peter's death by martyrdom impelled his followers to feel superior to John's followers, whose master lived to old age. The words of Jesus, in that case, would have given divine sanction to John's not being a martyr.

Those who think the passage had to do primarily with the delay of Jesus' return suggest that it was designed to dispel the anxieties of Christians who had actually believed that John, as the youngest disciple, would not die at all, but would greet Jesus' royal return. In Matthew 16:28, Jesus told the disciples: "Truly, I say to you, there are some standing here who will not taste death before they see the Son of man coming in his kingdom." And, significantly, this was part of the passage about Peter's confession of Jesus' messiahship and Jesus' giving him the keys of the kingdom (16:13–28). In other words, Peter's commissioning and the word about someone's living until the return of Jesus were connected in Matthew as they are in John.

But John defuses the question, whatever its motivation, by saying that Jesus did *not* say to the beloved disciple that he would not die, only that it was no business of Peter's if he did say that (v. 23).

John's own view of the Second Coming is usually different from the view often held by early Christians. His emphasis was on the constant union of believers with Jesus and the Father, not upon a visible return of Jesus to earth. That is the point of the appearance narratives in the Fourth Gospel: Jesus comes to his followers as they worship and eat the eucharistic meal. They are not to pine for the end of the world and a new age. A new age dawned with the coming of Jesus and the imparting of his Spirit. Eternal life is a possession of all who believe in his name.

Guilty, Lord. I am guilty of having waited to see what others would do for you. What if you had waited for someone else to love me and die for me? Forgive me, Lord, as you forgave Peter. And use me in whatever way you wish, for your kingdom's sake. Amen.

Week 12: Saturday

John 21:24–25 The Final Word

We come at last to the second or final conclusion of the Gospel.

"This is the disciple who is bearing witness to these things," says the writer, "and who has written these things; and we know that his testimony is true" (v. 24). "The disciple" is the one described with Peter and Jesus in verses 20–23, namely John the beloved. The "we" of the second part of the verse suggests that at least this final passage, if not the entire twenty-first chapter, was written by an editor. His reference to John is in the third person: "his testimony is true."

Perhaps this writer was one of John's disciples, and, in ruminating on the stories of Jesus he had heard John tell, decided that the ones in chapter twenty-one should be added to the Gospel originally written or dictated by John himself. Therefore he appended the narratives of the fishing expedition, the meal at the seashore, the commissioning of Peter, and Peter's asking what John was to do.

And, when he got through, this nameless disciple imitated the conclusion in 20:30–31, attesting from all the stories he had heard John tell that there were countless narratives yet to be told. In fact, he said, the world itself could not contain all that might be written.

Suppose all these things had been written. Would it make the lordship of Jesus more credible? Probably not. "The Jews" had not believed, even though they saw many of the signs and wonders occur in their very midst. One of the points often made by the Gospel is that faith is a gift, and no one can believe who is not drawn by God to do so (6:44).

But what wonders those who are drawn do see!

Do you remember the calling of Nathanael in chapter one of the Gospel? Nathanael was astounded that Jesus knew him under the fig tree. "Did that make you believe?" asked Jesus. "Wait until you see the heavens opened, and the angels of God ascending and descending on the Son of man!" (1:50–51, P)

Before the Gospel narrative was over, Nathanael had seen this. He had seen Jesus' oneness with the Father, and the way Jesus' Spirit could bring that oneness among the disciples themselves. He had seen a man raised from the dead, blind men given sight, lame men made to walk again. He had seen the risen Christ in the midst of the disciples, showing his wounds from the crucifixion and causing a skeptic like Thomas to cry out, "My Lord and my God!"

In other words, Nathanael's way of seeing had been completely transformed. He no longer saw a mere man who had extraordinary powers of personality—he saw the very presence of God, as though heaven itself were opened and angels were ascending and descending on the Son of man!

This is what the Gospel is able to do in our own lives if we believe. It is no ordinary book, for it is about no ordinary life. Its theme is life eternal, and it has a power to change everything for us, if we only believe in the One at its center.

"Have you believed because you have seen me?" Jesus asked Thomas. "Blessed are those who have not seen and yet believe" (20:29).

That is our cue. We are the ones he was talking about. And this Gospel has helped to make it possible. Because John bore witness, and talked of some of the things he had seen, we can believe too. We, like Thomas, can exclaim, "My Lord and my God!"

How wonderful, Lord, was the witness of John! He has made me see and feel and understand things I did not know. Grant that I, in turn, may be the kind of witness he was, and share your life-giving presence with my world. For you are the Resurrection and the Life, and there is none like you; no, not one. Amen.